Kisses of the VIRGIN

Chibesa Emmanuel

authorHOUSE®

AuthorHouse™ UK
1663 Liberty Drive
Bloomington, IN 47403 USA
www.authorhouse.co.uk
Phone: 0800.197.4150

Published by AuthorHouse 04/12/2016

ISBN: 978-1-5246-3031-7 (sc)
ISBN: 978-1-5246-3032-4 (e)

Author's notes

This novel is strictly for the elders! No kids' stuffs. The content of this novel is based on a highly romantic true story. However, names of places, institutions and people have been changed and any similitude is just a coincidence, thus, I solemnly disclaim any form of damage suffered in whatever form it might be.

See also a movie.

DEDICATIONS

The first dedication of 'Kisses of the virgin' goes to you Priscilla Chanda; my academic and spiritual friend for over fifteen years. I wish you good health and happiness as you advance in your career.

The second dedication of this book goes to Mr. D. Mulenga; my senior secondary school teacher of English. Learning English from you at Mungwi Technical School is the best thing that has ever happened to me in my academic endeavors. You gave me an instrument with which to defeat poverty and make the impossible possible. 'Kisses of the Virgin' would also have been totally impossible without the peculiar knowledge of the queen's language I tapped from you. For this reason, you will remain close and highly treasured in my heart for all the days of my life.

The third dedication goes to you Dr.Felix Chibesa-Ubwafya, Ottenel Tembo, Temba Saina, Granton Bwalya, Ailedi Kabwe and Blessings Museba. I hope my secrets are safe, eeh? Don't ask me why have asked such a silly question. You are the only seven people have shared my secrets with. And to you Temba Saina; thanks for having taught me the game of chess, eeh! I promise you heavy hitting next time we meet, that day we shall hit the bottle up to the last atom of our strength.

And last but not the least, special dedications goes to Joe Sabi, Isabel J.M.P.Mwale and Reverend Steward Kabaso; some of my few acquaintances in the school of law at Zambian Open University(ZAUO). I best assure you brothers and sisters that the little education I fetched from ZAUO is being put into good use, especially in my writing career. In particular, this book would have been totally impossible without the peculiar knowledge in Communication Skills and in General Principle of Criminal Law I tapped from ZAOU. Anyway, what is knowledge if it can't reproduce; if it can't help us make sense of the real world; if it can't help us make the best out of life. Anyway, why go to school if not to come and reproduce what we learnt?

The final dedication of this novel goes to you my fellow teachers in Zambia: Kachacha Mutondu, Chali Godrick, Mtonga Alick, Kabungo Henry, Mwape Henry, Lizazi Jacob Malimbu, Chilala Collins, Linda Muhoho, Milimo Agustin, Chanda Mafupa, Chanda Stenslous, Jane Luanga, Kalenga Kelvin, Sichiyanda Kaubi(SK), Mutale Angel, Chizongo(too good for a teacher), Musonda Maybin, Mazala Biggie, Mwelwa Chingi, Siwila Keddrick, Namusokwe Brenda, Kasonde Martin, Shimulope Alexander, Chama Lillian, the list is endless, but for lack of time and paper I will end just here.

PROLOGUE

The billion dollar question is: What makes 'kisses of the virgin' sensuous, scintillating, titillating, tantalizing, irresistible and compelling to read? It is Surriana! She was born out of wedlock; a product of an adulterous woman. At the age of twelve, Surriana was abandoned by her parents and left to be brought up by her grandmother until she was fifteen. But one day, Surriana decided to cut and run. And from that day onwards, she started living on her own.

Regardless of her upbringing, Surriana grew up to be a very extravagant beautiful and stunning woman. Her body was attractive and as enticing as a motif from Abraham's symphony; she had an interesting back and nice long legs, her breasts and nipples were pointed and well positioned, and her wide generous mouth was a promise of sensuous kisses. She had long natural hair that reached up to her knees-as black as the nimbus clouds-and as silk as silk hair can be. Every time she walked, she waved her hips professionally such that men always found their mouths wide open-thinking of nothing but sex. As a general ensemble, Surriana was the perfect feminine equipment a man could ever dream of taking to bed.

For a blonde of her type, it is odd that she was still a virgin at the age of thirty. She had done everything an extravagant beautiful blonde at her age could do with men, except that one thing-sleeping with them. She was warned by Bana Chimbusa (her traditional teachers) never to take men to bed-and she adhered to that. But one Bright summer afternoon, she met with Chinuel, and from that time onwards, strange things began happening to her until she was compelled to lose her virginity, that one thing she treasured most, that one thing she had vowed to Bana chimbusa not to lose until her wedding day. Worse still, she was subjected to imprisonment, blackmail, murder, pain, sufferings and sexual abuse. As if that is not enough, she was impregnated and left to look after the daughter alone.

CHAPTER 1

Surriana: Meaning, 'a practical joke.' Her birth is as unique as her name imply. In fact, to say her birth was a practical joke is to underestimate the circumstance in which she was born. But for lack of better terms, I will say, Surriana was a product of circumstance, a lack of a condom, a child born out of lust-a child born from the maggots. An offspring of two people with lust that could make a dog vomit and the kind of libido that could sicken a pig. Most unfortunately, I will not go into much details of Surriana's early childhood, but right from here, I will pick it up when she was at the age of ten and cover much of her sexual life until her age of thirty.

At the age of ten, Surriana was already something for the top birds only. She was stunning and intelligent. While I'm on that subject of intelligence, I would like to add that Surriana had all the seven levels of intelligence: Musical intelligence, Love of beauty (aesthetic intelligence), spatial intelligence, linguistic intelligence. What else, name it and I will tell you she had it. In short, Surriana was holistically developed; those in the education sector know what I'm trying to insinuate.

And when you talk of physical beauty, Surriana had it. Well, you have already read that stuff in the prologue, but for emphasis, I would like to repeat a number of it. Her body was attractive and as appetizing as a motif from Abraham's symphony; she had an interesting back and nice long legs, her breasts and nipples were pointed and well positioned, and her wide generous mouth was a promise of sensuous kisses. She had long black natural hair that reached up to her knees.

Surriana, what she used to do and say was surprising for a girl of only ten. Not that she used to do and say disgusting things, all the things she used to do and say were things strictly for the top dogs. In other words, she used to do and say elderly stuffs. Take for instance this one bright summer morning; Surriana wake up early in the morning only to find her dad (if you could call him that) on the Veranda reading a novel.

"Don't you ever get bored with that?" She asked him.

"Only that I have nothing better to do."

"Mum says breakfast is at ten. If we hurry we can take Talwaka for a walk," she said pointing to the dog.

Killan Mwana Cosma rubbed the dog's chest to let him know he'd been noticed and the exuberance subsided.

"Anything you say," Killan said. "Did it rain last night?" Surriana shook her head.

"Pity, Talwaka would like that."

"He has seen the rains before. He is as old as I am." She said and went back in the house to wear her running shoes.

"No need of reminding me about that stuff," Killan snarled.

Outside the weather was surprisingly chilly. The wind had changed direction and a wave of coldness swept through Surriana's body. She shivered.

"I don't like the cold," Surriana said, straining to keep up with Killan's strides.

"Do you like the cold?" She asked.

"Not if I can help it. I prefer the rain to coldness.

"I have noticed. Don't forget I have been with you in summers and winters." She said and smiled cheerfully.

He laughed. "Yes, not like your mother, she loves it when it is cold."

Surriana thought for a moment. "Do you love mum?"

"Not as much as she does!"

"Then why do you stay with her?"

"It is only because she is my wife."

"Do you like acting the party of a husband?"

"Some of the times," he said.

She wrinkled her nose as she looked up at him, her expression deeply curious. "Have you ever loved any other woman before?"

Her question took him in times of yore. He remembered that morning, that only day he had cheated on Sheila. Most unfortunately, it had to be with the boss, Jane Bwinga.

Killan Mwana Cosma had a business to discuss with his boss. They met in her office. They talked in a stiff manner which left no room for camaraderie. After that, they had coffee together. Then from without, Jane said; "do you believe in that old rule that says, a good business is followed by good coffee, and good coffee is a sign of good sex?"

"And what if it is true?" Killan asked.

She laid down the cup and stared directly at him. "We play by the rules."

"What does that mean?"

"Come on, Mwana, you want me and I need a man. This time it's for free, next time, it'll cost you–and a lot of it."

Killan lifted his hands and let them fall heavily on his knees.

"I want you, Jane, but not on those terms," he said, quietly. "I've never paid for it and I never will."

She stared at him, and then smiled.

"I think I'm going to like you, Mwana," she said. "I think you're all man. No conditions. Let's see how swell you really her."

He got up and putting his arm around her waist, cupping her heavy breast, he went with her into the tiny bedroom attached to the office.

The wave of paralysis swept through is body as he remembered that violent love making with Jane in that office. He had taken her with all his lust, increasing each force of thrust. She had cried like a pig, but when he had stopped deliberately, she had requested him to continue. Although she had failed to contend him, he had enjoyed every moment of it.

Remembering that day; Killan clapped his hands and murmured to himself: "Some days are sweet." Then, he looked apologetically at Surriana.

"That's a very personal question, kid." He said to her using strictly B movie language.

She shrugged and walked on. "I understand if you don't want to talk about it. Mum doesn't like talking about that sort of things." She sounded very grown up.

"Especially on a bright day like this one," Killan added pointedly, trying to discourage her.

"Mum never wants to talk about love. Never! I mean if you don't love someone, there's not much point in staying with him or her, and there is no point in being faithful to him or her, is there?" She asked him and took a deep breath.

Killan almost stopped dead in his tracks.

"God knows what is going through the child's mind. But how do you tell a child of only ten, what Love and marriage are. or that at times, people who used to love each other and spend much of their time together would at one time just end up giving each other a pain in the ass every time they are together, but they have to keep up together for the sake of the children. Anyway, a child who believes in Father Christmas wouldn't be able to believe that, why bother telling her?" He thought.

"Is there," she repeated the question.

Killan frowned. "This conversation is getting a bit deep, kid, hop it!"

"If that's the way you feel about it." She said and that's how the all conversation ended. No talking until they came back to the house.

CHAPTER 2

Surriana's twelfth birth day was just like any other day, except for one thing; the family was expecting Banda Greedman, Killan's best friend. Sheila (Surriana's mother) planned to dust off with him. And when the time came, she talked Banda into it. It took a long time, and as easy as breaking a rock with an egg. Sheila liked men like Banda who kept their stance on a given subject. She always knew where her position was with them. The only trouble with Banda was; he was always one jump ahead of her all the time. But she was prepared for that. She timed it so well such that she caught him unaware. Anyway, she sold him into it in the end. Why bother with the details, what is important is that Sheila foxed Banda into scramming with her.

Well, just a brief account. Banda arrived early in the morning, only to find Surriana standing on the landing, one hand poised on the banister, with the morning sun behind her transforming her long hair into a golden halo. As she stepped down, rays from the sun played over her *face. It was inevitable that she would be smiling that warm open smile that made Banda feel like he was the most welcome person in the world.*

Banda found his own mouth responding involuntarily, twisting into a boyish grin as he noticed how extravagantly beautiful Surriana had become.

"Hello, Uncle Banda."

Banda nodded. "Surriana......" He was aware of his own hesitation as he searched for something to say. "I hear that congratulations are in order?"

"What for; if I may ask?" She protested.

"You're now a full grown up lady."

She pouted mischievously. "You could say that although I'm not sure dad would agree, but all the same thanks."

As she reached to hug her, he almost pulled back. She noticed and a flicker of uncertainty showed in her eyes. "And thanks for coming, uncle Banda. We were beginning to think you'd abandoned us. It's been so long. The last time you came was when I was seven."

Banda noted that Surriana maintained old-fashioned, middle class value of politeness and etiquette, which he rarely came across in kids of her age. It was a bit traditional and reminded him of his own, more traditional background in the village.

Banda Swallowed. "I've been busy kid." He said using strictly B language. "You know how it is with Business, especially with the falling of the Kwacha every day."

"But couldn't you find a day......"

Sheila intervened. "Well, he's here now."

"Welcome Banda," Sheila said and Shook hands with him stiffly, then led him to the kitchen where Killan (Sheila's husband remember, and Banda's best friend) was waiting in an apron.

"Welcome home, you son of a dollar," Killan exclaimed as soon as he saw Banda. "It is good you came; there is a lot of work to do."

"Then it looks like reinforcement as come at a right moment. Can I help?"

"First thing first though my dear boy. A drink, Whisky and ginger wine suit. You could do with it if you came in that open-topped contraption of yours, and then a good sleep." Killan said happily.

"Straight scotch thanks." Banda Greedman said and smiled.

In as short as chicken sex, Sheila brought Scotch.

Killan watched her pour Banda a glass then said, "We've been married for fifteen years now, Banda, and she never ceases to amaze me. Now that she is up she will take total command of the household, the cooking, everything. I can think of a couple of business men who could do with a lesson from Sheila on organization techniques."

"That is probably the nicest thing you have said about me in this year," Sheila murmured.

"Banda sipped his drink, his mind preoccupied. He vividly remembered what happened twelve years and nine months ago. He had called around to the farm to see Sheila whilst Killan was away. Sheila had suggested that the two of them take a picnic in the mountains. It had been a perfect day. Warm but not too hot, with the air sweet with pollen and bird songs. Wine from the cooler went ideally with the brie cheese and grapes.

They had made love on top of the mountain on a very huge rock. It had been spontaneous, starting with the touching of fingers. He'd never known such a simple act to stoke such fires. As he clasped her hand, their faces had moved closer. As though it is something they had agreed in advance. Their lips closed and they kissed. Their kissing had been long, sluggishly, and abandoned. And before he realized what she was doing, she had her pants off. No guilt for her. He took her in the only way he knew how to take a woman. Then later, she had plainly wanted him then and there. It surprised him the way she was crying out, tearing his back with her nails, he knew then that his best friend hadn't spent time coaxing her as he should. Perhaps it had been an act for his benefit or rather doing him a favor–if there are such things.

When it was all over, she had brushed her panties back up her legs and as he also hauled up his trouser awkwardly, strands of grass caught in the zipper, she laughed and helped him remove them.

When he looked at her, there had been fierceness in his eyes. "I've wanted to do that for a long time."

"I know." She said and smiled provocatively.

"Since when?" She asked.

"Since the last Christmas, if my memory is still servicing me well."

She looked at him as if he was a nice piece of art. "I've always liked you, fancied you maybe, then the last Christmas, that lethargically kiss under the tree when I wanted to grab your walking stick, remember. Anyway, not all gifts are under the tree, some are in the heart."

"I should have stopped coming......now it as even comes to this." He barked.

She had frowned. "This we've done, that's all. Don't go all guilt about it."

"Anyone else, but my best friend's wife, it is a curse."

Again she had frowned, "well, as I said forget it, I wanted it badly too. In fact, you have done him a service; Killan is in love with his silly book writing, Banda. Books see more of him than me, and that's saying something. I love him dearly.......and I know he likes writing, it is in his blood–but I'm a woman and needs sex than he needs it, so don't feel sorry for him on that account. You know something? I thought this was the golden land of opportunities when I landed here three years ago. Was I green? I spent two years in Ndola in the hospital, nursing sick people. God! Was that a bore! Then I got a transfer to Kitwe, the same old bore. Then one day.....my unlucky day.......when I was fed up to my back teeth, I had to run into Killan, full of plans of starting a publishing company, writing is own novels, in a year writing three, in three years a lot of books... famous and stinking rich! So I married him! Okay, I asked for it and got it, we came here. "Give me a year, and you'll see. Let rough it for a year, he said. "That is three years ago, and what a man!

What a man to live with!" she looked directly at Killan. "He's Kinky, high heels and whips. So we sleep apart. He gets his fun writing and I get my fun cooking.

Four months after Banda had gone; he had received a letter from Sheila. It was short. It read:

"Dearest Banda,

For the fact that you always take the largest part in my daily memories, there comes a greeting that proudly expresses affections and best wishes for your health. Thanks for the visit; I'm looking forward to another one. I'm expecting a baby girl, Killan thinks it's his, but only the mother knows the real father of the Child. Remember that day in the mountains; I knew it will come to her. I plan to call her Surriana, as you know it was all just a practical joke.

I send you my love, hugs and kisses.
Sheila."

Banda's memories Jolted back to the present. He wondered how different Killan's reaction to him might be now, If he suspected that the child he so dearly loved was not his but a product of someone he had trusted like the fox that was trusted to look after the hens.

"*Could he ever forgive me and Sheila or could he......*"
He thought.

His thoughts were interrupted by Killan. "*Hey bud, you have scarcely touched you drink, anything wrong.*"

"*Nothing, I guess I'm just toiled up. I will do with a good sleep.*" he said and stood up.

The afternoon burst like a barmy thing to Banda Greedman. It took him a few minutes to orientate himself to the sloping ceiling of the tiny dormer bedroom. He glanced at his watch on the bedside table. Holy Tembalake! It was almost fourteen o'clock. He fell back on the pillow.

"*The party will be on soon,*" he said to himself. "*I have slept like a corpse.*"

There was a timid knock at the door, and he sat up as it creaked open. Surriana stood in a long nice white dress, clutching a mug of coffee in both hands.

"*Are you awake, Uncle Banda?*"

"*I am now, thanks.*"

"*The party starts at 14:15, just thought you should know.*" Surriana said more of a woman than a girl of only twelve.

"*Call me dad,*" he wanted to say but kept the words to himself.

"*After the huge traditional party, Banda offered to do the cleaning up while the rest of the family went shopping. Just as the family assembled into some kind of order alongside the land Rover, Sheila announced that she wasn't feeling well.*

"What's the problem, love," Killan asked. "Not sick again?"

"A bit queasy, it is expected, especially after a time like this, I had slaved myself to make this party a success."

Killan smiled. "Unusual for you, though. Better stay behind, eh? I'll bring you a coffin plus a nice dress for your funeral."

Sheila hit him softly on the shoulder. "Don't bank on that one; I expect I'll be over it by the time you're back. But just in case I die, promise me that you will let mum take Surriana."

"You have yourself a deal!" Killan said and coaxed the cold engine into life and in as short as chicken sex the Land Rover was out of sight.

Slowly, Sheila turned back to the house. Banda Greedman was already halfway through the washing up. He turned, "I thought you were going together? It is nice to see a family together."

She let the question skip and for a moment a silence formed between them, broken only by the sound of water and the clacking dishes. Then Sheila said suddenly: "Does it make you feel awkward Greedman, being alone with me again?"

"Damn you bitch." He wanted to say, but instead he said casually, "not at all."

"So, you still care?" A teasing smile played around her lips.

It was several second before he took his hands from the sink and turned to face her directly. "Unless someone deliberately hurts you, I don't think you ever stop loving someone who's really meant something to you. Not if it was ever real."

"Do you mean; true Love is forever?"

"That's it. To be honest I'm soul into you–but for Killan, I would have taken you places."

She smiled provocatively and stepped towards him.

He wanted to scream at her not to step towards him, but his tongue was tied. His muscles were paralyzed as she slid her arms along his, her long fingers curling around his neck. And then her lips were brushing against his. Memories flooded back. The firm moist flavor of her mouth, the way she played her tongue along his teeth. It was all the same, only more exquisite than the last time. That a kiss could make even a corpse come back to life.

His resistance crumbled and the madness seemed to possess him. He took her in his arms, his hand cupping her breast, he sucked on her lips; first the upper one, then the lower one. He sucked on her tongue and he drew saliva from her mouth into his like a desperate motorist sucking petrol from a drum with a short hose-pipe into the tank of his vehicle.

In his arms, she thought her body felt gelatinous.

His hands dropped to her waist, his fingers caressing her leftovers. But feeling that was not enough, he stooped down a little and the hands went under her dress, then under her half-slip and then rested on her panties. His mouth was all the while grazing her mouth and the two of them seemed to be doing a rocking dance. He went down on his knees in front of her and threw the front of her dress over his head. She gripped his ears tightly and began to pull hard as if she meant to snap them off. He deflowered her and helped her to lie on the kitchen table. He looked at her and saw that she lay with her eyes closed, her luscious round thighs still partially opened and inviting.

They had made love like two lost lovers in the jungle, enjoying every moment of it; knowing that when it is over they will have nothing interesting to do.

When their passion had subsided, Sheila said suddenly: "This time you will not leave me, will you? I will go with you. I love you, I want to spent the whole of my remaining life with you, I'm tired of having boring days with Killan, he no longer makes me feel a woman, he is a selfish character."

"If that's the way you feel about it, I'm all yours."

"Let us scram before he comes back, shall we?" She said smiling; not believing it could be so easy, as easy as putting fertilizer in the vegetables.

"What will happen to our little mother, Surriana?" He asked. "You know Killan is no good to take care of a small kid like Surriana."

"I will write to mother, I'm sure she will understand and she will keep her safe for us. I will be sending her money from time to time until she is old enough to take care of herself. But for the while, I also want my on fun and scramming with her could be no fun, but a curse. Mind you, we only live once, and I want to make the most of it. Besides, menopause is at forty-five."

When Killan returned from Shopping in a Land Rover filled with things, he was surprised to find Banda and Sheila gone. There was a small note on the table. It read:

"I thought that I would spend the all of my life with you, but how foolish I was. You are no good to any woman. You have never learnt how to care. Luck enough, I have just found someone who has learnt to do just that–and I don't give a dime if he is your best friend. I have scrammed with him. You may as well know that Surriana is not your child, she never was. Mum will come to pick her up."

Later that afternoon Killan was alone in the room, staring out at the falling rains, when Surriana came up to her.

"Daddy!" She shouted.

Absently Killan reached down and ruffled her hair.

"Daddy, will Mum and uncle B be coming back?"

Killan looked as though mesmerized by the fading landscape. "Not today, not ever. But your grandmother is coming to pick you."

Surriana felt rejected and abandoned. "How would my own mother leave me for good without even saying bye? Worse still, why should my own father send me to the village when he is still alive?" She thought, but didn't say anything.

CHAPTER 3

When Surriana's grandmother realized she was going to have a very attractive granddaughter, she decided to equip Surriana with Knowledge and means of self defense. She knew too well that in this modern world, attractive young girls wouldn't remain virgins for long unless they went around the streets with their eyes wide open, and their legs closed.

At the age of thirteen when Surriana had her first menstrual period, her grandmother organized for her, an initiation ceremony.

This initiation ceremony started with a ceremonial song:

> "Mwana wandi na kula eya (call)."
> Senimumone yanga yanga (response).
> mwana wandi na kula eya (call).
> Senimumone yanga yanga (response).
> Mwana wandi na kula eya (call).
> Senimumone yanga yanga (response)."

Meaning my daughter has become of age, everyone come and see.

This was followed by women dancing in a sexual provocative manner: swaying, swinging, and rocking their bodies—like they had no bones.

"Should I undress for her," one old woman shouted.

"Undress for her, Nakulu Mulenga, Ukufunda umwana kufikapo" (a child needs to be taught fully), the women responded to her in their local language which they all spoke very well.

The woman ripped naked and every one became silent.

"Surriana, have you seen this happening before in your life?" The naked woman broke the silence.

Surriana failed to look up and answer. Not until she was threatened to be beaten up by are grandmother did she make the effort of looking at the naked woman.

"No ma!" she answered apologetically.

"I have done this not to disgrace you or the elderly people around here, but to show you that from today onwards you are my equal, you have become of age. This is a welcome to the club. You have to realize that if you have this and it is ripe you will be a game to men." The naked woman said while pointing to her leftovers. "There are lots of poachers outside there, hunting for your virginity—even right now. You'll have to learn to protect yourself, or else, you will not make it up to the wedding day; virginity is something that a real lady keeps for her man. A real girl does not lose her virginity until the day of her wedding, no matter what!" Bana Kulu Mulenga advised her.

After that, Surriana was taught the facts of life and some few tricks about satisfying a man in bed. "You will soon learn that a man gives love in order to get sex and a woman has to give sex in order to get love. A man requires sexual fulfillment before responding to his wife's need for affection, caring and romantic attention." Surriana was told.

"Kissing, embracing, petting and fondling mark the beginning of a fulfilling love making," Bana Kulu-Mulenga continued. "While I'm still on this subject, I would like to add that the caressing of a man should be done sluggishly and lovingly, and should include all areas of the body, not only areas directly related to sexual excitement. It should include caressing of the inner thighs, lower back and the buttocks, earlobes and back of the neck. This gives an indication that you are not just interested in sex but in him as a whole man. When your husband makes sexual advances, you must know that he is asking for more than sex. He is asking that you accept him. He is looking for emotional closeness. Sex may be the only way he's ever learned to get close. To a man sex is another channel of communicating love to her wife and if you do not give it to him, that channel of communication is broken." She paused.

"Alalalaala........ala.......ala..... ala," the women ululated. "Kokolapo, Kokolapo!" They shouted. "Mushebwa aile namafi kubuko (She who was never taught went with shit to her in-laws)."

The naked woman smiled chotalically and then continued. "The first sign of effective sexual communication in your man will usually be the erection of the penis. Until that happens will he enjoy a gentle massaging of the scrotum? You must be careful not to apply excessive pressure to the testicles. When he is fully aroused tempt him in, but never suggest it to him directly. Always and I say always make him feel like he is the one taking the initiative."

What followed was a loud noise mixed with clapping and ululating. Then her grandmother started singing and dancing alone:

> *"Seke seke na kupandila,*
> *we mwine ukayonene,*
> *Seke seke na kupandila*
> *we mwine ukayonene."*

Meaning: "Honey bird, have given you honey, you will just destroy it yourself."

Surriana was then taught how to take care of her sweet-self during menstrual periods, and shown how to cook palatable traditional dishes. While still on the subject of cooking, she was advised: "If you want a man to stay at home, Cook him nice meals and always make sure his stomach is full. China lucelo ulemuma akamwiko pamala Umulume obe (make sure that your husband is given something to eat every morning). Another thing, never put salt in the relish when you have gone to the moon, do not ask us why."

Better still, she was trained in skills associated with self defense. And by the day she was returned home, she was wiser and more equipped with life.

Then her final day came; the exhibition day. The exhibition started late at night in the light of the full moon and the camp fire. Young men and women from all walks of life gathered around the camp fire, eager to watch the 'Nachisungu' dance and drink the katata (local beer) that goes with the exhibition performances.

At last, the old women came at the camp fire, each one carrying a clay pot full of katata on the head-not holding to them. In their hands they carried branches of leaves. They sang and danced:

"Twingile shani eee,
twingile musense nga bakolwe,
Twingile Shani eee,
twingile musense nga bakolwe."

They went around the camp fire three times, dancing like they will never dance again: their waists bend down, while their buttocks were shaking as fast as lightening, and their overused breasts followed the rhythm of the song; kapa-kapa they quivered, up and down, up and down.

They entered the small thatched house in which Surriana was hidden in fashion. Instead of the normal way, they entered in the single line and with their buttocks first, throwing the branches of leaves on the roof as they entered.

A wave of silence swept in for five minutes or so, then suddenly the women in the house shouted: "Ubukwebo bushimoneka tabushitwa (goods that are never advertised cannot be sold)!" Then Surriana came out. But for the small strip of Chitenge cloth that covered her small pointed breast and the other that covered her leftovers, she was naked. Her coffee brown body was shining with increasing glossy in the light of the moon. She walked mwambalically, like a chameleon, taking care of each step-as though the ground had ice. She was throwing her nice long legs methodologically as if she had all the time in the world.

As she approached the arena, the drum beaters started beating the drums. The rhythm that came from those drums was something, something that could make even the old persons feel like they are only thirteen, something that could make even a dog dance, something that could heal the sick.

Surriana put on her best performance, a dance of her own invention-her knees on the ground, her waist bent outwards, her hands on the ground. Probably, this was the most sex driving dance ever performed in Chikwanda village. Men found themselves in a bad position, their penis erect; some had even wetted their panties.

"Ukupesha chibola kumoswela," they shouted and whistled.

Well, this reminds me of something. Do you know where Chikwanda village is? It is that scrap of a place located twelve kilometers away from Mpika city. It is along 'The Great North Road,' so, if you use that root, I'm sure you will not miss it. But just for the sake of some more details. Once you start off from Mpika City, just know you have even reached Chikwanda. Just count the bridges. The first one is Malashi River; the second one is Lwitikila River. That is where the Chikwanda women draw their water from! Just drive a little, you will find a sign post of Chikwanda School, drop there–if you want to see me, you are already in Chikwanda. But if you are coming from Nakonde boarder, that's different. All you have to do is; when you reach 'Danger hill,' keep your eyes to the left, you will soon find a poster that says, "Lwitikila Girls High School," drop there and look to your left, you will see a house some few yards away–that's my mother's house." Talking about this village cannot end without saying that, long time ago, it was a place for the mad people only. And that it has a popular waterfall by the name of Lwitikila waterfall. It is said there used to be a very big snake, or sorry; ichililomba–whatever, at the waterfall. It looked like a white man and it had long raven hair. But that was in the nineteenth century–this time things have changed.

Well, back to the initiation ceremony of Surriana. When the dance was over; her grandmother covered her with a very big Chitenge cloth almost hiding her, then, women came from the house with the clay pots of katata which they distributed to people around the camp fire. And as they were drinking, the man for the last words stood up.

"Before the world was polluted and over populated, it was also called a virgin," the old man began. "By then man had only one enemy, and that was loneliness. Any woman who would help a man get out of his loneliness was said to be capable of keeping a man. But now that the world is old, polluted and over-peopled; there are ten rules that a woman needs to follow, if she is to keep a man. And these are:

"1. No nagging, silence is the best torture.
2. Never refuse a man sex, not even after a squabble.
3. Good cooking makes a man stay at home.
4. Always make sure you are well dressed. A well dressed Woman is a pride of a man. Make a man always feel attracted to you, and for this reason I suggest that you always be modern in you dressing-try to wear clothes that are short, tight and appealing. In this way, you will spare your man the temptation of looking at other women.
5. Understanding, patience and tolerance are the only medicine to a falling relationship.
6. Charming words, a provocative smile, good sex and lots of respect are the only keys that unlock the wallet of a man.
7. Share the bed, Love and Food with your man, but Keep secrets to yourself. The less he knows the safer for you and the more you talk about yourself the

more you risk being dropped. Always remember that the main reason why God gave us two ears and one mouth is because God wanted us to be doing much of the listening and less of the talking.

8. *Always know that people we love do not love us as much as we do, so if you find yourself in a position where you love a man but he does not love you much; just be content that at least love was able to grow in you.*

9. *Once you are out of your parents hands, you become a 'Mrs.,' meaning a 'Man's Registered Servant;' so be royal and humble to him.*

10. *Do not let your man become to close with your female friends and your young sisters. Chikwi tapalamana na mulilo (dry grass cannot get in contact with fire without getting burnt)."*

"If you keep these Ten Commandments then your man will not run away," he said and sat down.

What followed was, heavy clapping, like thunder. Indeed this was talking rich; almost everyone liked every word of it. But Surriana didn't like the ninth phrase. "I thought my husband will be a friend, now this stuff of being a servant, I don't like it at all costs," she said to herself.

It was around mid-night when the exhibition came to an end. By then, everyone except Surriana was drunk.

CHAPTER 4

Surriana had her first kiss when she was at the age of fifteen. Unfortunately, it had to be with Pastor Kabungo. Worse still; in her grandmother's house. Don't get me wrong when I say unfortunately, I don't mean Pastor Kabungo was a bad man. In fact, everything about Pastor Kabungo was spiritual and orderly. Everything he did in a day was planned for; that is everything from his personal shopping list to his appointment diary. Each minute of the day was planned for, as was all money in his bank account. Even the maximum number of words he would be able to articulate in a day was planned for, and that is to say he was a man of few words. He was a man who never left anything to chances; it would have surprised his church members to know that he had even arranged for his own funeral in the event of his unexpected demise, so as to spare them the distressing task.

Pastor Kabungo had an appointment with Surriana's family, to share with them the gospel of Christ, but to the devil's good luck, only to find Surriana alone. She had received him politely and sat with him on a two-seater sofa which was the only seat in the house. She sat so close to him that her knees touched his and when he seemed to want that contact, she had put her hands on her knees and drew even closer, and faced him. The Chiffon dress she was putting on was short and tight, so tight it was that it showed the all outline of her body.

As the man of God was preaching the Gospel of Christ, she became absorbed, so, she became careless and her legs parted. Lusaka and London is as apart as her legs were. He looked under her; she had coffee brown thighs, nice thighs. Worse still, the underpants she was wearing were as white as white underpants could be. Then she looked at him. That look made him uneasy. Surriana knew how to pick her grounds. She knew too she was making an impression on him.

"Jesus loves you and he wants you.....to.....to......to be his.....fre.....Fre.... friend," Stammered the man of God.

"How Pastor?" She smiled and rested her hands on his thighs. She did that with innocence.

"If you believe that.........that.... that....... that........"

"What Pastor?" She asked and smiled provocatively, her hand still on his thigh.

"That he......that.... he...," That was the end of the message. He threw the Bible on the table.

"Damn you." He said as his hands dropped to her waist.

For a brief moment, she surrendered to the pressure of his body. Her sharp and pointed breasts rested on his *chest. Surriana had never felt as passionate as she felt. It was like there was an electrical spark between them. She smiled provocatively, so he gave her a quick killing kiss. When he drew his lips away he was surprised that her's was still slightly parted. He kissed her again, this time more passionate. He felt an erection as he teased her tongue out of her mouth and squeezed her breasts methodologically. Then his hands went under her chiffon dress and rested on her favorite white panties, his fingers manipulated her leftovers while his mouth was all the while sucking her saliva like the way a bird sucks nectar in a flower.*

As if to show that she was in total agreement with him, she had mooned delightfully and wriggled her sex body, pressing herself more tightly against him. He had put his hands on her head and ruffled her hair. It surprised him the way she was also holding him tightly, digging his back with her nails, beating his tongue with her teeth and moaning delightfully. This gave him an indication that this was the first time she was being coaxed.

She mumbled something breathlessly in his ear. It was then that something snapped. He pulled back.

His voice was hoarse. "That is enough; let us not lead ourselves into sin."

She clutched his fist in her hands. "God, Pastor, I can't tell you how much I have enjoyed this. I know it is wrong—at least in the eyes of the Church. But it feels right, I mean you being a Pastor. It is my luck day."

Pastor Kabungo turned his head from side to side as though seeking some means of escape. "If it is going to be like this, Surriana, then I can't ever see you. Not after what we have done together. I can't afford to betray God."

Her eyes pleaded. "And me, what about me? Don't my feelings enter into it? I mean, if you praise God you have never seen and hurt a friend, is there a point in being a man of God, is there pastor?"

"You're not quoting the bible on this, and that really is not the true meaning of that verse." Pastor Kabungo snapped.

She shrugged and sat up. "I understand if you don't want to have anything to do with me."

Pastor Kabungo frowned. "God, this conversation's getting a bit deep, young lady, But to tell you the truth, there is nothing in the world I'd like to do more than to take you now. On this sofa; here in the sitting room because I want you more than I've ever wanted any girl in my life. I want to take you in the only way I have known to take a woman."

Her eyes narrowed as though not quite believing. She appeared to tremble.

"But It's not possible, Surriana," he added, his voice fractured. "I belong to God. I made a choice long time ago, for better or for worse to follow him always, and never to fell into sin, especially with a kid like you." He said and took the bible and kissed it.

"May my God give you peace," He said and left.

Surriana just gasped and then covered her mouth with her hands.

For two months after the first incidence, Surriana had no chance of having Pastor Kabungo by herself. They always met in public places–with people. Then, the break came. Pastor Kabungo, Surriana and five other Church members went to visit a Church member, who was sick. As they reached the stairs, the other five members moved fast leaving Surriana alone with Pastor Kabungo. She saw her opportunity; she deliberately skipped, pretending to fall down. In no time, Pastor Kabungo was on her. He grabbed her. For five minutes or so, they remained like that, and then Surriana turned and planted her lips on him. In so little a time, they had kissed more than they had kissed on the first incidence.

When it was over, Pastor Kabungo had yelled: "Oh, my living God! Not again."

"Help me God," Surriana managed to say.

Five days after the second incidence, Surriana received a letter–if you would call it that, from Pastor Kabungo. It was flat out, it said:

"It is either you or me, but God tells me, one as to leave Chikwanda Village. And I guess I have more things to do here than you, so, that puts you into a fix."

When Surriana read that letter, she cried bitterly, cursing the day she was born. What she wouldn't understand was what made the man of God hate her–so much that he wanted her out of her own village.

This page is intentionally left blank. It is for you Brother Kelvin Mataka Chibesa Ubwafya. Not because I forgot you on the dedication page. I just thought a full page may do for my heartfelt congratulations. Your graduation with a Bachelor of Commerce from Mulungushi University made me proud. Anyway, what are brothers for if not to make us proud?

CHAPTER 5

For two more weeks after the last incidence with Pastor Kabungo, Surriana Still kept up with her grandmother. Then without any warning she packed her bag and left. She had no misgiving and no regrets about it. Surriana was ready to carve her initials on opportunity's door.

She had made all the necessary plans. Her first move was to pilfer her grandmother's cash. Then she wrote her a note. It was cut and to the point. She wrote her that she was tired of living the hard way and she wasn't to worry about her. She told her why she had taken the money. She didn't think she would miss it, but thought she had a right to know.

She put her bag on her back and headed south. She wanted to get as far away as she could from Chikwanda village. She had seen the pictures of Lusaka city and she wanted to go there. Now there was nothing to stop her.

She arrived in the evening, a few minutes after eighteen hours.

Surriana watched a black and Chromium Benz turn into the Cairo road and slid to standstill by the narrow passage that leads to kamuchanga market. Except for Surriana and two young women, the road was deserted-one of those things that sometimes occur in the streets of Lusaka for no apparent reason. The two young women regarded the Benz with professional interest and also, perhaps, with a feeling of bitterness and envy at such a display of wealth. Surriana and the two young women watched the slim looking man leave the car and look helplessly up and down the street.

"Think he wants us?" The taller of the two women asked the short woman.

"You are not in the Benz class," Surriana who was some few distance chipped in.

The slim man noticed them talking and approached them.

The tall woman said, "Hello. Did you want me?" She was secretly surprised to see how young he was now that she could examine his round immature face. In spite of his immaturity, there was something about his eyes and the rigid way he held himself that made her uneasy.

The slim man looked at her, recognized her for what she was and made an imperceptible movement of disgust. Except for her noise, she was a smasher; something worth paying for. Something for the top dogs only, something that every man worth his salt would want to take to bed.

"*Do you know where the 'Linda hotel' is?*" *He asked after a moment's hesitation. His voice was soft and timbreless.*

"*Holy Tembalake!*" *The tall woman exclaimed, angry in her disappointment.* "*Why don't you ask a policeman instead of wasting my time? I thought you wanted me.*"

"*There is no policeman to ask,*" *he replied, hating her with his eyes.* "*Anyway, you don't look so busy.*" *His thin mouth twisted in a sneer.* "*If you don't know, say so and I'll ask someone else.*"

"*Then ask someone else,*" *the shorter of the two young women said, trying to help her friend.*

"*Yes, ask else were,*" *the tall young woman snapped, still sour with disappointment.*

"*Ask me,*" *Surriana said, joining them.* "*I know,*" *she added as an afterthought.*

The slim man looked suspiciously from the tall woman to Surriana. "*Well, where is it?*" *He said impatiently.*

"*I'll take you there if you make it worth my while.*"

The tall woman heard her. "*Why. Holy Tembalake!*" *she exclaimed, suddenly angry that she herself had not seen the commercial opportunity.* "*You don't know where it is any more than I do, you're a stranger here, I saw you when you were coming out of the bus.*"

"*Oh, yes I do.*" *Surriana tossed her head.* "*I keep my eyes open and my ears to the ground. I saw it as we were coming in the Bus, and I can take him there if he can make it worth my while.*"

"Hop it, cheepie!" The tall woman snarled. "Can't you see you're in the way?"

"I like that," the shorter woman said bitterly. "We spoke to him first."

"Don't be silly." Surriana smiled, but her eyes were cold and threatening. I know where the hotel is, you don't. He can afford to give me something, but there's nothing for you."

"So you know where this hotel is, my pretty?" He asked.

She nodded, and then added, "I will take you there if you give me something."

"What a clever little thing, just like all the Zambian women, always looking for money. Alright take me there, I will give you one hundred kwacha, only don't waste my precious time."

"Make it two, darling," she returned quickly, "with such amount I will even be nice to you along the way."

"A few minutes' drive is not even worth a hundred. I am just doing you a charity."

She eyed him. "It's not my time you're paying for. It is my knowledge."

He smiled again. "Just as I said, just like all Zambian woman. Anyway, so it is."

She brightened. "I didn't think you were mean," she said, fluttering her eyelids at him. "I'd like it now, not that I don't trust you, but a girl can't be too careful."

"It is all a question of money if you're in Zambia, isn't it?" He returned. "Here, perhaps you will have more *confidence if you have this." He gave her two hundred kwacha.*

"You're a foreigner, are you?" She asked as she slid the dough into her purse, but her eyes never left the roll that remained in his hands.

The tall man nodded, "we will drive there."

The tall man opened the door and they got in.

Surriana gave an ecstatic sigh as she sank into the cushioned settee. It was, she thought, like sitting on a cloud.

"This is marvelous," Surriana said, as the car slide away. "I'd give anything for a car like this."

The tall man seemed not to hear her, "You did say you will be nice along the way. Will you allow me to paw you as we go?"

"As you wish," Surriana replied apathetically.

He held the steer wheel in one hand and rested the other hand on her thighs, caressing her with it–as though he was searching for a lost needle in a dark place. Then his hand went under her favorite Chiffon dress. Surriana gave a sigh of relief and smiled to him. Deeper and deeper his hand went slowly, but when his hand reached her nylon panties and carelessed her leftovers, she turned quickly and slapped him on his face."

"Sucker, that's the only one place you don't touch," She snapped.

The Benz nearly got off the road. "Sorry I didn't know."

"How would you, she answered and then laughed." Have I hurt you?"

"Something of that kind," he said.

The remainder of the drive was in silence, and no pawing. Then, Surriana pointed to a sign post. "The sign post is this one. I guess you can find your way from here."

The tall man killed the engine and Surriana got out.

"Take care Sugar," the man said as he engaged the gears."

"You too," she returned, blowing a kiss at him.

That is how Surriana earned her first money in the City. As simple as that, and just like all the Zambian women-they like easy dough.

The next day, Surriana Banda walked down Kafue Avenue and paused at the corner of Chipata bar as a car cautiously edged into the stream of traffic flowing toward Buntungwa square. A man said out of the car, "hello, girlie, going my way." Ten tax drivers had said precisely the same thing to her during the past hours.

"Well, you might not know me very well, would you?" The man in the car continued speaking very quickly. "Just to give you my ABC, I'm Honcy, The owner of this bar you're seeing," He said pointing to Chipata Bar.

"You might be a power house to your mother, but to me you are just a five letter word." She sneered.

"Come on, I will fix something for you, anything you say." He said and then laughed Mulebalicaly.

Surriana was thinking fast. "The owner of that bar did you say?"

"*Eee Sure yee!*"

"*Could you have any Job for me then? Anything, I have had such a rotten day; I have searched for a job the all day but with no luck.*"

"*Just like all the Zambian women, always looking for a job,*"[1] *he said and laughed.*

"*If you don't have anything for me say so and I will ask else were.*" *She said full of rage.*

Honcy was a very wicked man, he couldn't just see something in a dress without making a pass at it. He was well married, but still claimed to be double single. It was said that probably Honcy was the most intelligent student teacher at Kitwe College of education and if he wanted a woman, he always got her no matter the costs. His motto was, "never leave fresh meat un-eaten." So, when he looked at Surriana, his mouth was wet with saliva. He had never seen something as beautiful as her.

"*Can you dance?*" *He asked. "I think I can use a piece of art like you, as an advertising instrument.*"

Without answering, Surriana Put on a little performance, but it was good enough for Honcy's eyes.

"*Geee, that was something,*" *he said and giggled. "You are in. Come tomorrow at 08:00hrs we discuss the wages.*"

That is how Surriana got her first job in the city. Just like all the Zambian women, as easy as calculating pure mathematics. For three months, she worked as a dancer in Chipata Bar. But one day, Honcy called Surriana to his office and when she refused to make love to him, he fired her.

---

[1] See also, 'Chibesa Emmanuel's Essays on Zambian Women.'

CHAPTER 6

For the next five years, Surriana stood on her own feet. Sometimes she worked in night clubs, but most of the time she just travelled from place to place within Lusaka city. Her bank was the wallets of chance acquaintanceships. When she ran out of money she found a sucker and picked his wallet. She was always careful. Her swift fingers were never detected. She could take a wallet, remove some little dough and put the wallet back without the owner noticing. More often than not, the money was never missed.

Ever since her childhood and until then, no man had ever seen her naked body. But one evening when she was twenty one, something happened which was to change her current records. As she was preparing to leave the theatre, there was a young man who wanted to meet her. He was a traveling salesman who had looked in on the town with the hope of drumming up some new business. In the evening he went to the theatre. He saw Surriana, was dazzled by her looks and came round the back intending to dazzle her with his money.

The young man's name was Chiluba Layman and he seemed a pleasant enough young fellow. Surriana went with him to a restaurant and had an expensive dinner. During the dinner, Chiluba did a fatal thing. He showed her the size of his bankroll. It measured an inch and a half round its waist. Surriana had never seen so much money in her life. He bragged about it. He told her that he had stacks of dough in the bank. So Surriana thought she did teach him a lesson and she lifted his roll. It was the easiest job she had ever done. Though she was only twenty one, she had kicked around. You don't work pick pocketing for five years without learning that ABC is invariably followed by D. She pulled on him the oldest, hoariest trick in the world. As she leaned forward to pick up her glass, her hand knocked Chiluba's beer into his lap. Before he could move, she was on her feet. She whipped out his handkerchief from his breast pocket and began mopping him. Thus, pilfering all is cash.

"I'm sorry," she stammered. Her face was scarlet with mortification. "I'm not really clumsy, has it ruined your suit."

Chiluba took the handkerchief from her and dried himself. "Accidents will always happen," he said feeling sorry for her. "Don't worry about a little thing like this one."

She lifted her hand to her nose and made a little grimace. "Mind if I wash?" She asked. "I'm all over beer." She smiled brightly at him and swept away from his table.

Two well-dressed men, sitting near them drinking Mosi were also interested in Surriana. They had been muttering to each other the moment they had seen her and now one of them pushed the chair, stood up and followed her. Egg-yolk blondes were his weakness and he couldn't let such an opportunity pass him by.

Chiluba whipped around, "don't get your-self in an uproar buddy," he snarled. "Repack your fanny! I'm not finished with her."

"Who said I will leave such an egg-yolk blonde to a punk like you?" The well dressed man said. "It is high time you scrammed off, you are using too much air in here. Besides, you give me a lot of pain in the ass."

If any other greaser had said that, Chiluba wouldn't have hesitated to pine his mouth on the ground. But he had superstition about hitting a guy twice his size; not that he had not come across tough greasers before, he had knocked around Lusaka city for some time and had faced plenty of tough men, but this one was something special. If he had to do anything, he did have to do it with a gun. That was the kind of a greaser he was. Unfortunately, Chiluba didn't have a gun with him.

Surriana didn't hesitate to push Chiluba into a fight. "I hope you are not going to let a man with no more brains than a stone insult you, at least, not in my presence."

"Uneven odd is a sign of chivalry," Chiluba said trying a new line of argument.

"I know you're just trying to sound off. You are shit scared of this greaser; you as well know that he will poke you in your panties like pig's business."

"I'm not just in the mood," Chiluba said sounding very annoyed. "Pipe down; it is ladies like you who cause revolution."

"The senior as milk in is vain." The greaser said and laughed up to the last atom of his strength. It was a well-defined laughter, mixed with matakalic pride. As a general ensemble, he was laughing like he had all the time on earth.

That set Chiluba on fire. He stood up and gave him a fast swift punch on the fore head. Though it didn't have much weight, it did something to the greaser. It did send him flying with a kind of craziness. He felt like he had been bitten by bees.

For a couple of seconds, the greaser man was in grievous pain. Then he came back to life. He fingered his pistol, pulled it and pointed it at Chiluba. "Get out of here boy, before I melt your scrotums with my rod. Take off-drift- scram-dust off-pissy off!"

Surriana anxious that there would be no further trouble came in between them. "Hello apple blossom," she said addressing the greaser man. "This is no good joint to shoot a man. It is loaded with law, if I was you, I did wait until I met my enemy in some places safer than here."

"All the same, I'm going to wreck this joint if he doesn't pissy off within five seconds. And just for the record: I'm a man who knows no law, a strange product of nature, a criminal without a crime. My true name is killer; I kill when I want and serve when I feel like." The greaser man said with aristocratic pride.

"I think I will like you an awful more than I thought." She said giving him her go ahead smile.

"A well-dressed man, a tough looking man, a man who totes a rod and a man who would wreck a joint within 200 meters from police national headquarter will always interest me." She said and pulled on her don't forget me type of a smile.

That settled him for some time. "Alright, but next time I'm going to shoot him and apologize to you later," Chomba said while putting the rod back in his jacket.

Looking at Chiluba with his viciousness and then at the greaser man, calm, amused and completely unflustered, Surriana felt a sudden change of heart. She realized Chomba was a man for her. The realization came as a shock to her. She wanted him to herself. Surriana was pretty blasé about men, but Chomba got her. I'm not saying she fell in love with him, but she liked him better than any other man she had met and she wanted him to be the second man to kiss her.

Surriana twisted around to Chiluba. "If you love yourself, run for your life, this man is not kidding. Beat it; there are enough corpses in this city without you adding more to the statistics."

That traumatized Chiluba, he felt bitter. He knew he had lost the girl and in as short as chicken sex, he was on the move.

Surriana and Chomba saw him go.

"Let's get out too," she said and started off. He followed her behind until she reached the parking rot. He found her looks disturbing. He didn't know what it was, but her metallic hair gleaming even in the dark, the column of her neck, the curve of her figure, her well calculated morphology, her nice long legs, her behind, her small finely boned hands and the courage of her mouth and chin got him crazy. He found himself groping back into the past to remember any one woman he had known who looked like this kid, but none of them clicked, not even in a movie.

"Where do I take you sister...?" he asked.

"Just a minute," she interrupted, facing him. "Would you mind not calling me sister? I'm no sister of yours. I've got a name, Surriana."

"It did have been good had you been my sister."

"All you tough guys think of is violence, that's the only sweet words you can think of, isn't it?"

"If only you knew half of what I've got lined up for you beach blossom, you'd be climbing trees," he said. "You will thank me before dawn blooms."

"What do you think I would expect, when you feed me with a hot tongue and cold shoulder?" She asked grinningly.

"Would you say I'm a serious man?"

"More than that, but I guess I'm going to know you an awful lot better before we wave good-bye." She said in her sweet and sex voice.

He caught her hand and pulled her close to him. She didn't resist, but let him pull her across the small space that divided them. He slid his arm under her shoulder. They stayed close to each other and he would see the overhead clouds reflect in her eyes. She made no effort to push him away.

"Will you like that?" He asked his lips close to hers. Then he kissed her, pressing his mouth hard on hers.

"Maybe–I don't know." Kissing her like that was as good as kissing the back of her hand.

She shifted away from him. Her finger touched her lips carefully, "you meant that to be something, didn't you?" She asked adjusting her remote dress.

"Sure," he said. "But what of it, some places, it's all right, but this place is no good for such." He said looking disappointed.

"The other trick is not to rush this kind of a thing," she said.

"How about having coffee anywhere away from this dreadful place," she suggested.

"That is an idea, what of my place?" He asked Chibatalically.

"I guess not, you are too dangerous to follow to your place, besides it is late." She said looking at him.

"Changed your mind about knowing me awfully well," he said, watching her intently? "Or are you just petrified of saccharine things I will do to you should you come with me?"

"Scared of what? I'm not scared of anything on two legs. In fact, I will like the experience, I have never been in a man's house alone, especially dark at night. But you will have to behave yourself. Don't come and say I didn't warn you. I'm a lot dangerous too."

"Then you better come," he said and walked to where his BMW was.

"I've thought about it," she said, getting into the car. "I don't like the idea any more, I smell a rat. Just take me home."

"Give it a try, he urged," as he engaged on the gears.

"I said my place and no fussy about it, or I will scream."

"Ok! If you get to my place I will give you this," he said producing a diamond necklace out of the dash board locker and spread it on her thighs."

Surriana took the necklace and studied it. The necklace was really a work of art. There was nothing as artistic as it under the sun. Surriana fell for it and that settled it.

"I hope for your sake that I'm not going to have any trouble from you at your place." She said, putting the necklace on her neck.

"Be assured of that," he said and increased speed a little.

"I have myself a meal. Brother! I'm going to enjoy this meal and I'm going to make the most of it." Chomba said to himself and increased the speed.

Miles and miles they went in silence. Then, Surriana broke the silence. "How I wish we could go on and on like this until the end of the world. Most unfortunately, that is *not possible. It is the divine plan of God that at one time or the other things have to obey the law of inertia; you not it? It is the tendency of the body to remain in its state of rest or if in motion to continue in its uniform motion unless acted upon by an external force."*

"That's Pure Physics, is it?" Chomba asked.

"Sure," she answered indifferently.

Ever been to a University, Chomba asked looking perplexed.

"Some of those things I just learn from the streets. I learnt that material the same way I learnt that a 'tortuous liability' arises from the breach of duty temporally fixed by law and this breach is toward persons generally and is redress able by an action for un-liquidated damages."

"You're talking like a lawyer," Chomba said even more surprised.

"Umwana ashenda atashanina ukunaya," she said in her mother tongue.

Chomba pulled up outside the front gate of his bungalow. The sight of the bungalow brought a lump to Surriana's throat. Its size, its design, the lawns, the swimming pool and the rose garden were all splendid.

"The maggot is not only extravagantly handsome, but he is also in cash- a lot of it." She said to herself.

He seem to have read her thought for he said; "the best thing you can do for the poor is not to be any of them, spend were you should and save were you could."[2]

---

[2] See also the same quote in 'The gospel of money' by the same author.

They entered the house and Chomba indicated a seat. He did this in a stiff manner which left no room for camaraderie. Chomba made two strong cups of Swiss coffee, which they drank with maximum enjoyment, without even, caring each other's presence. But by the time they were through with coffee and on wine, they had become so free with each other such that they began saying and doing things they would not do in their sober state.

It was Surriana who started it.

"Are you married?" she asked abruptly.

"No." He answered affirmatively.

"Do you have a girl friend?" She smiled fleetingly.

He hesitated for a moment, not sure whether he liked her direct approach or not. He was not one of those men who were fond of revealing such intimate details about themselves to all sundry.

"Not anyone you will come to know of," He said frankly.

"And you," he asked.

"Sileki Bamudala!" She answered in her mother tongue.

"I thought a blonde of your kind would have bunches of men chasing after you."

"It is good you just thought! How about having me as your first better half?" she asked and walked to his sofa. Her saunter was so provocatively such that Chomba found himself watching a little too intently.

He started appraising her. Though she was not a smashing beauty, she was a woman in her on special way;

she was attractive, no doubt about it. She was long limbed with well groomed and terrific hips, her cheeks were plump and as nice as nice cheeks could be- and they were as smooth as that of a baby. She had nicely rounded face and a pair of white sex eyes which appeared watery and shy. Though her breasts were well hidden in the brassiere, even a common observer could see that they were good sizable products- fixed at their rightful position, her nipples stood stiff like soldiers on the assembly. She was wearing her favorite 'red chiffon dress'[3] which only went as remote as her knees. And because it was fragment tight, he was able to see the prints of her nylon panties. Her juicily and sex driving buttocks were also some form of exhibition in that dress. She wore no half-slip, and this made the slit to put her sensational thighs on display. He felt an erection; this made him even more an easy.

"That sounds like a swell idea!" He said and moved closer. He touched her long raven hair and looked into her dove's eyes; he saw that she felt it too. He touched her hand and as if his head had a will of its own, it moved closer until their lips touched. She tried to push him away but he resisted. He held her tightly and then kissed her tenderly. Then, the kisses became lingering and deep, as he realized that she too was enjoying the act.

He kissed the sweat that ran along her neck and his mind reached uncontrollable peak. He pulled the dress off her, unclasped her brassiere; almost tearing it and yanked

---

[3] See a red chiffon dress worn by a woman on the back cover of this book.

off her moist panties. He looked at her luscious rounded thighs and his penis seemed to bust.

She suddenly came to her senses and tried to resist, but she was nearly too late. He had held her down on the sofa and told her she shouldn't struggle.

"Leave me alone sucker!" Surriana pleaded.

"Take it easy baby. When I do it to you, you will be asking for more-and there is more were those passionate kisses came from, mind you." He told her.

"But I don't want to lose my virginity, at least not yet and when the time comes I will not lose it to a punk like you." She said and gave him a warning look.

"No one keeps it forever, not even Mary the mother of Jesus." He whispered.

There was no hesitation; he pulled off his slack and made a grab at her. Surriana was in no way flustered, in fact, she was most anxious to find out whether the advice her grandmother had drummed into her when she was thirteen really worked.

As he made a grab at her, she swung her arm and hit him squarely under his nose with the side of her hand. She had been advised by her grandmother never to pull a punch. The chopping blow she handed out to Chomba was thrown up to the last atom of her strength and had all the stamina behind it. The side of her hand landed accurately. The blow broke Chomba's bridge-work, made his eye water and sent a thousand red-hot needles into his brain. Then she gave him a kick between his legs and that did things to his balls. He fall down and when she touched him, he had already kicked the bucket.

Immediately Surriana realized that Chomba was dead, she planned the best method of getting rid of the body. It hadn't been very easy, but she did that alright. She had set fire to the building. It had been carefully done to look like an accident. After setting fire to the building, Surriana had started running, without panic, into the darkness. It was only after several minutes, when she paused to look back, that she realized she was still having Chiluba's money and Chomba's necklace.

In the secrecy of her bedroom she counted the roll. She found that the evening entertainment had netted her twenty Thousand kwacha (twenty million kwacha in those times) and a lucrative necklace. She didn't sleep at all that night. There was much to think about. She made her plans before the dawn light filtered round the window blind. She planned to buy a new car and move to another town, to make sure there was no chance of Chiluba seeing her again. She separated the notes into two even packets. One packet she put in her bag, the other she folded neatly and slid down the bottom of the pocket of her underwear. Then she took a large scale town map and studied it. "Livingstone is my next hunting place," she said to herself and relaxed. In just a trivial time, she was dreaming having a party in hell with demons.

The next day, the local paper dutifully reported that the forty years old business man had been found burned. No further investigations were carried. In fact, the *police were more than happy to see him blow his last breath. Chomba was a reclusive millionaire who fueled the opposition party, except he made a lot of his money through drug dealing. He was untouchable drug dealer that the police had wanted touched, but they didn't have where to begin from.*

The time came for her to pack and move to Livingstone. She arrived, rented a small flat in Dambwa North on a seven years lease–nothing very special but she liked it, being a person with no ambitions of getting married and having a family. She settled and began her operations.

To put you more in the picture, I'll give you a brief idea of her daily routine in Livingstone. She got up late and over coffee she planned the menu of the day. She believed in eating well, but at the low expense of the various self-service stores in the district. Surriana had dreamed up a smart idea of getting all the food and drink she required, not only for nothing but without risk. She had made a lightweight oval shaped basket with an open top which she strapped to her tummy. Over this she wore a maternity dress, her make-up pale, she looked the part of a brave little woman about to have her first baby. Not only did she jump all queues, but she lulled all suspicion while she stowed away in the basket the best cuts of meat and the necessary accessories that goes with a good meal. It was a nice racket and provided her with food for nothing. While she cooked lunch she read items in the post newspaper which she considered of interest. After lunch she worked the falls, dipping the tourists who came to see the Victoria

Falls. She was living decently, but with no ambitions to get rich.

In the evening she would go to the Cinema. If she was luck, as she always was, she picked a sucker there who gave her money in the hope of sleeping her one day, but she was always careful not to invite any to her place or to go to their places. She would go home late in the evening with enough money to eat on and a little saving for the rainy days. There was plenty to work on, but she kept her operations small and always careful not to have anything to do with the police. She would then watch TV until bedtime, and the following day would be a repeat of the previous day. Not what you could call an exciting way of life, especially for an extravagant beautiful and stunning woman like her, but it suited her.

For the next seven years she maintained the same routine. Always careful not to fall in love, she had totally no interest in men, but all the same they kept chasing after her and loading her with cash. They tried all their tricks, but she wouldn't play. You may wonder why men kept on pouring money on her despite the fact that she never gave it to them. Well, I'll give you a new photo of her. At the age of thirty, Surriana was sensational. There was no skirt on earth as attractive as her. She was a looker-with a traffic stopping figure and a pair of legs that caused car accidents. Her back was something; something that made men wet their panties, something that made the blind see and the crippled walk. Every were she went; it was third world war-with her as the root cause. Every man who *looked at her fell for her and begged to take her out and if she refused, he would not be discouraged. They gave her money in the name of amazing her, but with a hope of sleeping her one day. Unfortunately, she just never played until she reached thirty.*

This page is also intentionally left blank. It is for you 'IK'. Loving you is the main reason I was born. Don't get me wrong, I don't mean it is the only reason I was born. But without that, my mission on earth would have been incomplete.

CHAPTER 7

You think the first man to screw a blonde like Surriana could be a man with a reputable background, not so? Well, you are in for a shock, In fact, a very big shock. Surriana gave it to a punk, a sucker, a criminal with a heart as hard as diamond. She gave it to a man as tough as Hitler, as lethal as a black mamba and as sinful as the devil. And that brings Chinuel in the scene. Chinuel! No one ever heard him called by any other name. He was a symbol of evil; a friend of all and a friend of none, a criminal without a crime.

Although he was only twenty seven years of age, he was a veteran in crime. Very few people, if any, knew all what Chinuel did. Apart from owning and directing the Local heroes Firm, he was suspected of having his hands in every dubious pie in the country. Some said Chinuel controlled the all Zambia; some said that he dealt in stolen motor cars or that he was the biggest receiver of stolen property in the country. Others winked knowingly and hinted that his money came from a profitable traffic in drugs; others said his money came from the royalties in those scrap of books he had written when he was in Darussalam, while others whispered, "he is a Satanist," but no one really knew.

Being the only child of an acclaimed international lawyer, Chinuel had an inter-continental education. He had had a Master of Philosophy in economic from Museums University in Darreselum. He then took a brilliant degree in law with Capricorn University in United Kingdom. He later took a post graduate diploma and a master of science in Forensics with Chibesa Ubwafya University in Zambia. He then went to The University of Kachasu for his Masters degree in Criminal management. When he was not studying, he was always travelling; in this way he became as knowing as Jesus, as deceptive as a serpent and as treachery as a fox. By the time he was twenty one, there was scarcely very few languages he wouldn't speak, few jobs he wouldn't handle and very few people- if any, who wouldn't fell for his tricks. When he was twenty two, his father had joined a firm in Livingstone specializing in criminal cases. Without wasting time his father brought him into the firm as his personal assistant. He had a flair for criminal law and quickly made himself indispensable. The heart attack that killed his father some four years later made him a senior partner and when the other two senior partners pulled out, he became the owner of the all of the local Hero's firm.

The firm was one of the most exclusive law firms in Livingstone. Its six hundred clients who frequented the *place had one thing in common…..they all lived by their wits. Some of them were more dishonest than others, but none of them ever have been called honest. They ranged from an armament king to a pimp, from a female impersonator to a high class prostitute–if there is such a thing, from former republican presidents and ministers to street beggars and from pastors to corrupted trade union leaders. Between these degrees of degradation, the clients consisted of motor car thieves, confidence destroyers, share pushers, society women with kleptomania, blackmailers, illegal diamond diggers, drug traffickers and the like. Over them all, Chinuel reigned supreme. He was a friend of all and a friend of none.*

The only problem with Chinuel is that he had always been over sexed. Women were necessary in his life and he had so many lovers such that he had even lost count of them. He spent nearly all his leisure time chasing after blondes. In fact, Chinuel was unselective, and that is to say; he wouldn't just see anything in a dress without making a pass at it. Women dwelt in his mind consciously and subconsciously the way death sometimes dwells in the mind of the timid.

On the other hand, women were also attracted to Chinuel as pins to a magnet or as flies to rotten things. Perhaps, his frank smile, his posture, his small but masculine body, his big rotten teeth, that nose, his sexuality and those crucifying eyes did the charm. Besides, Chinuel had a terrific personality. His wide grin made you want to grin too. His laugh was infectious, his confidence in himself enormous. He was tall, slim and always well dressed. His fine pencil moustache made ladies gasp. Although he was hard, without scruples, shallow minded, selfish and a big liar, you couldn't help liking him. He was always smiling, always ready to crack a joke. He knew most of the famous people in the country by their Christian names; others said he was also on first name level with the republican president. He knew all the tarts, the playboys and the gold diggers, the rich fox, prominent politicians-and they all liked him. He was a typical conman and womanizer, and he didn't care who knew it. Others called him master, others called him teacher, others called him state Counsel, others called him 'local hero,' others called him a writer of our time, others called him Pastor, others called him investor, others called him donor, while others just called him friend. As a general ensemble, Chinuel was a man of many identities, a friend of whole and a friend none.

Just to give you a photo of how vicious Chinuel was with women; let me give you a scrap of that scene he was in several years back in Darussalam.

What does a man worth is salt to do when two nice looking women show up at his apartment, at the same time, begging to be coaxed? Well, the way Chinuel did it is; he made sure that each didn't know about the other and kept them in separate rooms. When coaxing one, he made sure that the other one was engaged in cooking and entertained by good music, and vice verse. When they were fully exhausted with passion, he had put some hypnotizing medicine in their leftovers. In as short as chicken sex, they were dreaming having intercourse with Satan in hell. He then slept them on one bed and continued with what he was doing, as if he had not been disturbed at all.[4]

---

[4] If you what to know what happed after the two women wake up, you can find the full story in 'Romances of Chinuel.' A Book within a Book called 'Third testament' by the same author.

CHAPTER 8

Well, back to how Chinuel and Surriana met. If he is not chasing after blondes, Chinuel spent his time shopping for nice cloths, in this way he was a looker. Surriana spotted him as he was buying himself shirts in one of the best stores in the tourist capital. She thought he was a real doll, but that didn't stop her trying for his wallet. There must have been something about Chinuel that spoilt her concentration because he felt her fingers slide into his hip-pocket.

He turned and smiled at her. They looked at each other and this chemistry thing called love clicked in her. She handed him back his wallet with a nice apology and accepted his offer for a drink. They talked for the rest of the afternoon until Surriana realized she should have been home an hour ago. This threw her into a panic. Not only had she been chatting up this handsome dude for hours, but she had neglected her afternoon work and had earned no dough, this she explained to Chinuel Who laughed and gave her one thousand kwacha (one million kwacha in those years and a lot of money by then) telling her he wanted to see her the following afternoon.

Surriana agreed to meet Chinuel in Miami bar the next day where they could eat, drink and dance. She had made no secret about what she did for a living. Chinuel had been genuinely amused and hinted he was partly in the crime racket too, although he didn't go into details.

It was while Surriana turned to go home that Chinuel had the opportunity of seeing her full figures and immediately he gave a long low whistle. "That's a nice bit of crackling, something resembling serenity," He said to himself. Surriana was also impressed and as he drove off in a BMW she said to herself; "not only is he handsome, fun and sexy, but he is also free with his money."

The next day in the afternoon, Chinuel was in Miami bar. Another of Chinuel's vices was hitting the bottle. He was a man who loved his bottle and most times, he would be in a state where his friends would wonder whether he would make it home. Miami bar was his favorite joint. Do you know were Miami bar is? It is that building along Chanika Street, just after Livingstone Museums.

Chinuel sat close to the counter, drinking Mosi. The bigness of the room hid him from the sun, burning up the road outside. The bar man, behind the counter, held an opener in his thick fingers. From time to time, Chinuel nodded his head to the bar man for a refill.

Chinuel uneasily fingered a bank note in his trouser pocket, it was his last money, and it was worrying him.

The rate at which he was hitting those bottles was wild. In as short as chicken sex, he was on his tenth bottle.

The bar man leant over the bar.

"Shall I fill you up, mister?" he said to Chinuel.

Chinuel hesitated, looked at the bar man coldly and suspicious, and nodded. He put the bank note on the counter. He did it reluctantly, as if the parting with it was a physical hurt. The bar man knew it was Chinuel's last money, but he wouldn't let him have one on the house. He was determined to have everything he could from him.

The bar man picked up the banknote, looked at it and flipped it into the cash box. Chinuel followed every movement with painful intensity. He jerked the chair round a little, so that he could see people walking along Chanika Street.

Surriana walked down Chanika Street. Conscious of the turning heads. Even bakaponya and the Mishanga sellers hesitated in their work, frighten to look up, but peeping, their heads lowered.

She clicked on, her high heeled shoes tapping swiftly. The men watched her, stripping her naked with their eyes as she passed them.

The women watched her too; cold, envious eyes, hating her. Surriana rolled her hips a little, she put on a slight strut, patting her dark curls. Her firm young body, moved rhythmically. Her full, firm breast jerked under the thin covering of her expensive, flowered sweater.

At the corner of the street, women stood in a huddle gossiping, ripping people to pieces in the hot sunlight. They saw her coming and stopped talking, standing there, silent, elderly, bulging women, worn out by child bearing and hard work. Surriana stiffened as she approached them. For a moment her step lost its rhythmic swing. The high heeled shoes trod softer. Her confidence in herself had no solid foundation; she was still young. In the company of her elders she had to force herself forward.

With an uneasy smile on her full red lips she came on. But the women, as she came nearer, shifted like a family of monkeys, turning their drooping shoulders against her, their eyes closed, not seeing her. Again the high heeled shoes began to click. Her face flushed, her heads held high, she went past.

A buzz of talk broke out behind her. One of the women said loudly: "She ain't got a thing under that Skirt, did you see!"

"If I were her mother, I'd skin her alive.......the little whore," the other woman snapped.

"Give her a Chitenge bana-chanda," another added.

"The dirty Sluts!" she thought, full of rage. "They know I'm young and fresh and they hate me for it."

At last, Chinuel spotted her coming and was impressed. He liked the way her dark shiny hair fell in natural waves each side of her small shoulders. He liked her doves' eyes; her well calculated morphology and particularly he liked her nice long legs, which he thought in his loose minded way would be sensational without cloths. Then, there were her provocative figures. He wouldn't understand how it was he hadn't seen her before in the club. She had told him *she was a member too and that she had been frequenting the club for nearly six months now.*

She came in with that confident air a well dressed, good looking woman has who knows she looks dynamite and is pleased about it.

Male heads turned to watch her as she made her way to where Chinuel was sitting.

Looking at her closely now, savoring her beauty, Chinuel had a surge of desire for sex he hadn't in days. He wanted to take her back to his pad, undress her gently and lay her on the bed. He wanted to take her as only he knew how to take a woman, slowly, spreading the pleasure until the climax came.

Surriana was quite pleased with herself. She had taken some trouble in dressing. She wore a black flowered sweater that showed off her breasts. Her white Mini-skirt was as short as the name suggests, and she knew it showed off her figure. There was scarcely a line of her body that he couldn't see. Her shoes shone. Her lipstick was vivid and put on to make her mouth look square, and her lips had a soft yielding look that made Chinuel feel short of breath. Her black long hair was piled high on the top of her shapely head and she wore flat gold ear clips and a gold collar around her throat.

He would have been startled and annoyed had he known that she had deliberately dressed herself in this way to appeal to his over-powering sense of lust. One of the club members had given her a tip that Chinuel was in big money and that if she played it cool, there was a lot of bread she would get from him. "If you don't open your legs for him, but allow him some few liberties such as pawing you, there is a lot of loot you could milk from him. Just play your card right and you will never be short of anything." She had been told. "Make sure you don't go with him in private places, Oh else, you risk being laid. And you know by now that once a woman gives in, especially so quick, she risk being dropped. The longer you keep a man dangling on a string, the more ardent he will be when you finally give in."

While he was studying her, Surriana had also examined him. He was in a black suit, well fitting, expensive and smart. The light was disturbing, but she could see his face well enough. He was young-she guessed, probably three years younger than she. His features were small and regular. His crucifying eyes held her attention-they were hard and experienced eyes-they frightened her.

Chinuel got her hand; kissed it and then ordered whisky. They drunk and chatted. Surriana's behavior surprised Chinuel. "Women are the weakest animals ever, especially with handsome men and celebrities," he had always considered, "and they are fun, especially if you have nothing to do." But this one was different. He could tell that. She was friendly enough, but there was a jeering expression in her eyes that irritated him. It showed plainly that she knew what he was up to, and was certainly not going to take him seriously. He could be as nice and as flattering as he liked, but it wouldn't get him anywhere.

This attitude intrigued him, as Surriana intended it to intrigue him, and he was continually trying to break down the jeering barrier she had erected to keep him at a safe limit. They had scarcely touched their drinks. Chinuel was vaguely disappointed, he had hoped to have got to know her better, but it was like trying to talk to someone behind a nine foot wall.

"Let's dance for the change," Chinuel suggested.

As they danced, one drunken man saw her. He thought she was the sexiest dish he had seen in years. The drunken man came close and grabbed Surriana's hands. "If you're bored with this punk baby come and dance with me, I will make it worthwhile," he said, using strictly x movie language.

"Piss off!" Chinuel snarled, his eyes turning vicious. "And make it snappy or I'll have to spank you."

The drunken man threw the content of his glass towards Chinuel's face, but that was old hat stuff to Chinuel. He moved aside and a girl coming up on the stage got splashed.

Chinuel jabbed a left into the drunken man's face and his nose exploded into a red mush. When Chinuel hits, he hits. The drunken man tried to back away, but Chinuel reached him a right hook that lifted him off his feet and slammed him flat on the floor.

The girl who had got splashed was now screaming like a pig and the rest of the people in the bar were shouting. It all happened in seconds. Chinuel caught Surriana by her arm and rushed her to the exit, and out into the hot night. She went willingly, stifling her laughter. He opened the door of his car and she got in-it was neatly done-no show of thighs. He slammed the door shut and before the club bouncer thought of moving into action Chinuel was driving away into the main road.

"If he can afford to run a car like this," she thought as they were safely away from the club, "he must have a lot of it; I'll see what I can get out of him."

"Wake up dreamy, where do you live?" he said and increased speed.

"Dambwa North, House number 303," she said while fastening the seat belt.

"What have you got-rooms?"

"It is a self-contained pad-whatever."

"Share it with anyone?"

"You surely want to know a lot, don't you?"

"Once a dick always a dick," he returned with a laugh and drove rapidly through the deserted streets. Neither of them said anything until they stopped outside her flat.

I won't waste time going into details; it's enough to say as soon as they were out and he had closed the car door, she threw her arms over his shoulder. He took her and kissed her like he will never kiss again. She responded like she was demented, but when he tried to manipulate her leftovers, she became offensive. She pushed him and started for the door.

"Hey! Wait a minute!" Chinuel snarled.

She paused and turned.

"What is the idea?" Chinuel demanded, puzzled, and he reached for her.

"Keep your dirty paw off me," she snapped. "We don't meet again."

"For holy tembalake's sake, lees go in. I could do with a cup of tea," he said.

"You're not coming in and you're not having any tea," Surriana snapped. "And if you want to see me again you have to pay me six million kwacha. Make no mistake about that."

He twisted round to look at her. He was smiling, but his eyes had hardened.

"But I want to talk to you. We can't talk here. Now be nice and invite me in, kid."

"I'm not in the habit of inviting men into my pad, especially at this hour of the night, just pissy off and make no fussy about it. And mind you, next time come loaded with cash–six million kwacha or you will not see me again."

He whistled softly under his breath.

"Have a heart kid! Where the hell have you got this six million kwacha stuff? You don't imagine I would carry such a large sum of money at this time of the night?"

"Six million Kwacha or you chance losing me to another sucker," She said and started off to the door.

For a moment Chinuel stood rooted, not believing what he had heard, then he got a rush of blood to his head and grabbed her arm and swung her around. He ran *into a slap in the face such that his eyes blinked and she wrenched free.*

"Holy Tembalake!" He Shouted.

"To-morrow morning or you lose me to another sucker," she said triumphantly. And before he could recover from the shock she had ran swiftly like a snake, opened and slammed the door shut.

CHAPTER 9

Chinuel waited long enough to see a light flash up a room on the ground floor of Surriana's flat, then, smiling to himself, he started the car and drove rapidly down the street. He hadn't far to go. He knew the city well; he found an all-night garage which was close by and left the car there.

He hadn't any trouble knocking off another car. It just stood in the main street asking to be knocked off. Even the engine was running, while some guy did is week-end store buying.

It didn't take him long to get to Malama stores-whatever it is-the place was almost deserted. He climbed out of the car, leant forward and took the ignition key; he ran across the pavement and entered the store, a gun under his coat.

A thin, security guard got off a stool at the far end of the store and wandered down when he saw Chinuel.

The security man said, "We're closing down right now," he sounded as if he was bored to hell with the job.

"*Grab some air,*" *Chinuel yelled, pitching his voice high,* "*this is a hold up.*" *The gun showed its black barrel.*

The shopkeeper was adding figures in a ledger, a skullcap on his head, and his face alive with intent satisfaction. He glanced up when Chinuel came in. "*what is it?*" *He asked, keeping one boney finger on the ledger page, nailing down a figure, as if he were frightened that it would escape him.*

Chinuel said: "*Stay where you are. Don't start a squawk. He held the machine gun so that the casher could see it. Chinuel shifted the gun a little and swung his fist. He hit the shopkeeper across his mouth with his knuckles. He flopped down on her knees and then spread out.*

The security man suddenly went yellow, and vomited like a two weeks pregnant woman. He didn't lower his hands, but just bent his head forward.

Chinuel walked to where the shopkeeper put the day's takings. He opened the till, pulled the drawer right out, found a bunch of notes, took them out and scooped them in his pocket. He said: "*Sorry bud, I guess I need this more than you, but for Surriana I wouldn't have dared to take your money, I believe in earning my dough. Maybe, when I get the breaks, I'll remember you, I will write you a cheque, but don't bank on it, Maybe it is just your fault, I hope for tembalake's sake you'll use a bank after this.*"

"*Don't start anything you will regret later,*" *he snarled at the security man,* "*this typewriter will cut you to hell.*"

He turned and ran until he reached the car. The car went down Linda Street with a rush. The quivering needle of the speedometer swung to hundred. Faintly above the swish of tyres and the scream of the wind he could hear people shouting. Chinuel gripped the wheel, his eyes fixed on the road that seemed to jump up from the ground and rush to meet him. Another car coming from the opposite direction crowded on brakes as Chinuel's car hurtled down on. Chinuel touched the wheel and swept by. The open road lay in front.

He hid the car in the woods some twenty miles from the town. He then walked all the way, back to Surriana's house.

For some minutes he stood outside, looking up and down the street. It was after 22:00hrs and nothing attracted his attention. Then, moving with confident ease, he swung himself over the iron railing guarding the basement of the house, caught hold of a stack pipe and climbed on to Surriana's window-sill. He pushed up the window and stepped into the room and closed the window. He moved with extraordinary speed and quietness. The whole maneuver did not take more than a few seconds. He pushed aside the curtain. The room in which he found himself was large and shabbily furnished and without much comfort. He guessed it was her sitting room. Across the room was a door that stood half open. The bed and the cupboard told him it was her bedroom.

After a few minutes, Surriana came from the bedroom and he watched her walk into the kitchen. She was now wearing an expensive sleeveless white night dress. It was cut so short such that it exposed much of her thighs. Chinuel *thought she was the most beautiful thing he had ever seen. So beautiful that he thought of her as a 'thing' and not as a woman. It was only a little later that he became aware of her sexuality. She walked sluggishly, waving her hips professionally, as if it was the only thing she knew to do well. He found himself watching her movement with more interest than the situation required.*

"This is all-woman," he said to himself.

The very idea of seeing such a beautiful and sophisticated woman going to cook made him laugh.

He stood for a few minutes, his mind active.

"Surriana must learn that I'm the coming man. No person slaps Chinuel and gets away with it. Nobody gets in my way. I get what I want no matter the costs. My true name is Mpinga, munshipingila ing'ombe yalya umulefwe. If persuasion fails only force is my answer. I'm killer, a strange product of nature. I destroy when I want and serve when I feel like; the only representative of God and a co-worker of the popes." He said with aristocratic pride and walked into the kitchen.

She came to an abrupt standstill when she saw him, and turned white, then red.

"Hallo, remember me?" He said casually and produced a roll of bank notes; he threw them on the floor, a distance from where she stood. She picked the money and counted it. "Twenty million kwacha, just enough to buy myself a nice car," she said to herself.

"Is all this money just for me, baby?" She asked him and put on her forgive me type of a smile. Her change of

expression toward him surprised him. It looked like the language of money is what she understood most.

"Think of it as nothing, some of those trivial things I do for symphonies like you."

"But Chinuel................."

"Make me some tea and make it snappy," Chinuel intruded. "I can't do anything until I've had some tea."

"You're the limit, Chinuel!" She said, weakening. "Well, Suppose I make you tea. I will not take time."

He fished out a cigarette and smoked while she made the tea.

She set the tray on the table and poured out the tea.

"What about that money, for charity?" She demanded as she handed him a cup.

"Now look, don't be inquisitive!" There was a slight edge to his voice. "I want you to make a little easy money and not to worry about the way you're making it. Are you not smart enough to understand that no man parts away with that sum of money without any hidden agenda?"

"Oh I see." She was instantly suspicious. "Laying me?"

"You're learning fast, six million kwacha a day for ten days plus a two million bonus at the end if you put on a good performance, I can't be fair than that." Chinuel said accenting each word.

"Six million kwacha a day for ten days and two million bonus at the end of it all, that would mean I would earn a total of sixty-two million kwacha." She thought. "And at this time such a sum is the pinnacle of my ambitions."

Immediately she made up her mind to get laid and cared less about losing her virginity. She continued thinking, "For goodness sake, don't start worrying about your virginity. You worry about money if you have to worry about a thing."

She considered: "You have only a few years on earth– another thirty with luck. What is thirty years more as a virgin without money, nothing and then the worms, the dark and the cold? All right then, I'm going to enjoy myself while am still alive, we only live once, but if we do it right once is enough. But I can't do it right without money. Money is next to God.[5] Money is power; it's fun, food, drinks, cigarettes, cloths, shoes and love. Money is a nice car, petrol, family, friends, children, education, health, respect, a lawyer and happiness. It is an air ticket, a night out at the theater and a nice house with nice furniture. It is everything good I can think of. I've tried working for a living, but it didn't come off. I have tried stealing but to no avail. And now I have this sucker around offering me so much money. I don't care what his conditions are so long as I get a hand on his dough, help myself. That's all there's to it."

"You're not pulling my leg, are you?" She asked him. "You could walk out of here after using me without paying me the outstanding dough........ I was not born yesterday."

He levered himself out of the chair, went over to stand beside her. "You think I will have it for mahala? I will pay

---

[5] See also a chapter entitled 'Money is next to God' in 'making the best out of life' by the same author.

you. I always pay my way. In fact, I like it in advance."
He said and produced a cheque, then, signed a sum of
twenty-five million kwacha (Twenty-five thousand
kwacha in today's money).

"Here you are, sweet blossom," he said and handed her
the signed cheque. "Hide it were even the black ants will
never find it."

"Holy Tembalake!" she snarled, "I'm not having any
of that. I'm not money hungry and I don't want to lose
my virginity. Not for money and not to a punk like you.
You get out, I'll chance being poor."

"You don't know your own mind, Kid." he said using
strictly B movie dialogue. "First you wanted cash, and
then I have to go. Well, I'm going to make up your mind
for you."

He jerked her around and slapped her face. He was
careful not to hit her too hard, but the slap was hard
enough to jerk her head back and her eyes became watery.

"I guess that is break even now!"

She was full of rage, her hand dropped on the kitchen
knife, but he caught her wrist, squeezed and the knife
dropped to the floor, then he caught hold of her, pinning
her arm to her side and shoving her out of the kitchen, he
forced her via the sitting room to her small and shabby
bedroom.

"Holy tembalake! Lee me go!" She exclaimed.

She was strong and hard to hold but he handled her.
He got her into her room, locked the door shut, and then
released her.

"Get them off or I'll rip them off!" He demanded in a metallic voice.

"Who do you think you're; a god?" She snarled her eyes blazing with fury. "I have never undressed for any man and I will never. Not for all the money in the world."

"I love that! But you'll soon have to, and for the start let us skip the singing and have some dancing." Chinuel said sarcastically.

To Chinuel who in the past had been in many brawls, she was pathetically easy. He weaved as she struck at him, her clawed fingers hopelessly out of range. Then he had her on the bed. Her wrist now gripped in his hand.

"Going to behave, baby, or do I really get forceful."

She stared up at him, and then relaxed. She knew that nothing would stop Chinuel having it his own way, even if it meant spanking her.

"I'll behave!"

He released her wrist and his mouth came down on her, for a moment she continued to struggle, then her arms went round his neck.

"Damn you! She said against his mouth and then, "you hold me tighter! Tighter! Tighter..........."

He pulled of her night dress and her stretch pants, and then his hands cupped her virgin breasts and placed his body against her delicious and soft body.

The next five minutes were the most exciting and exotic moment in Surriana's life. With her naked buttocks against the hard rough mattress, he did take her in a range of passions with little finesse, until she felt the sweat *running between her shoulder blades and the soft squelch of damp were their bodies touched. Their love making was long, tender, flexible, passionate and abandoned.*

He rolled off her and kissed the sweat that ran between her breasts. She laughed and ran her hand through his hair. He held her closely in his strong arms and in no time, she was having sweet dreams.

The next day, Chinuel came awake with a start and looked at his strap watch, and then he relaxed. The time was 06:00.......

"Plenty of time," he told himself and looked at Surriana, sleeping by his side. Her long black-natural hair half covered her face and she was making a soft snoring sound as she slept.

Cautiously, not to disturb her, he reached for his pack of cigarettes on the bedside table, lit up and dragged smoke gratefully into his lungs. The more he smoked, the more he became absorbed in his thoughts. "Friday is the delivery day of the largest kilos of drugs in the Zambian history. If I played my cards right, I did be stinking money." He thought of all that money in that deal, ninety-million Kwacha. "If I'm successful with that deal I will retire from the firm in six months. My first three months will be fair, then I will slow down, appearing to lose my grip and knowing my clients very well, they will look around for something better. In the sixth month I will retire and sell the firm to any sucker who will be dammed enough to think it is a profitable racket, then I will scram to Darussalam."

Thinking of Darussalam, his heart jerked with joy. The three years he had been there had left in him those unforgotten memories of the view of the Indian Ocean, the culture of the people, the sound of the pajar-jars, the food, and the all fun idea of trying to learn the Swahili language. The memories of Darussalam hunted him like the way the black ants hunts for termites.

"I don't think Darussalam could be as nice as it was without Surriana by my side," he said-half loud and half to himself.

"I will pull that deal and then take Surriana with me, who knows she might even accept to marry me."

He looked at the time and saw it was 07:00hrs.

"The right time to do things to her," he said to himself and lifted the bed sheets that covered her nakedness.

Without cloths she was a smashing beauty, a killer of men, a temptation to any man, a dish that no man would resist, one in a thousand, a vicar of beauty, a rose flower found among wild flowers, the most decorated piece of art, and as a general ensemble, her attractiveness was over-welcoming and next to none.

Surriana stirred and half sat up.

"You want coffee, honey?"

Her voice sounded lazy and sleepily.

He stubbed out his cigarette and leaned over her. "There is still plenty of time for that," he said, his fingers carelessing her leftovers and she sighed happily. This time she came willing, like a lamb about to be slaughtered. He did sweet things to her that she had never felt before. She had taken his in hers, and what followed was a quarrel between the two organs, with his trying to go as down as it can, while she also pushed hers upwards and her buttocks were dancing, shaking, swinging and swaying like a cement mixer.

"If sex is as sweet as this, then I have been missing out something and missing it on a big scale. This makes me feel a woman," she said to herself.

Later, as they lay side by side, she said, "This is probably the best thing someone has ever given me in years. Of all those that are sweet you're undoubtedly the sweetest. You're something sweeter than candy. No one else would have made me feel this way. You have rocked my world."

"That is what they say to a dog and feed it poison," Chinuel whispered in her ears.

"If you don't believe that, you will not believe anything." She said and smiled weakly at him. "You have bleached my heart with a bleach of love and affections that can only be felt for a man like you. My heart beats for you–and for you only. Your name is music to my ears and it flows in my arties instead of blood." She ran her fingers down his back. "I love you and a lot of it. You're all man. And from now onwards whatever you say, whatever you do is all right with me."

She slid off the bed and went away.

While he dressed, he heard the sizzling sound of bacon cooking. He went in the kitchen. Surriana, naked, was cracking eggs into the pan. Chinuel eyed her soft, luscious buttocks. He came up behind her, his hands cupping her breasts, his body against her softness.

She slid away from him.

"Skip it!" She said her voice hard. "We can't spend all this day just fu*****" She used the ugly four letter word and it shocked Chinuel.

"Take it easy, he said. This is a game of sex. I have paid for the full day, mind you."

"Stop it, Chinuel, or we don't eat."

"Mwebana lyeni, ine ndelalila ninenwe." He said in his mother tongue, at the same time grabbing her.

"You will hurt me, I'm not wet."

"You better be now," he returned as he entered her from the back. Her hands holding the sink, her waist bent, her leftovers pushed outward, she received him. There love making was a decimal thing. In as short as chicken sex, Chinuel spilled. Like a hose pipe, full of pressure. Surriana felt weak and poisoned. She stumbled and then sat heavily on the floor.

As they were having breakfast, Surriana asked, "Are you pleased with my love making," eager to be praised.

"Sure! Who can't be? Unlike those oversexed and overripe women I bump into sometimes, you've made me feel inside a woman." Chinuel said and laughed up to the last atom of his strength.

She had never suffered from jealousy before, but now the thought of any other woman knowing him as intimately as she did tormented her.

Seeing that she was hurt, he added, "you need not to worry, they are not as pretty as you."

"Don't tell me you are married," she asked.

"What if I'm?"

"Does your wife know you take lovers? I mean hasn't she ever suspected?"

Chinuel frowned, almost surprised that she didn't understand. "Kabwe loves me, Surriana. If she suspected anything she would never say. Her philosophy is a little like mine. She knew what I was like before we married. She's very understanding."

Surriana's smile lacked humor. "Then she's more understanding than I am; my husband, with another woman. You belong to her."

He swallowed hard, his eyes not living her. "It is not like the way you put it. Your line of thinking is silly. You have to realize soon or later that love is a natural gift–God's gift to us all. We must be true to it in whatever ways we can–by being true to ourselves. And I do what I know I have to do to be true to myself. I belong to no woman, Surriana. I never have. I love Kabwe as my wife. At times I have loved others, because I am a man. But I have never deliberately hurt Kabwe, never."

"What if you find your wife with another man, what could you do?"

"That is different. Ubuchende bwamwaume tabutoba ng'anda (A man's infidelity does not break marriage). I did divorce her. Oh no! Not that, I did kill....., not that again, I did just make sure she died poor. No, that is not

it. For all the temptations on earth, Kabwe cannot do anything like that. I trust that bitch like the fox that was trusted to look after the Chicken, she is as pure as rains and as perfect as the full moon."

CHAPTER 10

꧁ꉧ꧂

Kabwe sat before the dressing-table, a loose silk wrap across her shoulders. Her skin was faintly red from the hot water of the shower. Chinuel jerked open the door and walked in. Kabwe looked at him and glanced at the clock. It was now 21: 00hrs.

"Where have you been for the past ten days?" She asked, laying down the comb on the dressing-table and came over to him. She sat on the bed, looking at him with glittering eyes. "I need some works. You have been away too long." She almost snarled at him.

Chinuel heavy face hardened. "I'm tired kid; I need to grab some air."

"Too tired, even for love?"

What the hell is this? He said. "Can't I get tired sometimes?"

"Not the way you're tired, she shrilled. "There must be some whore with hot panties giving you the works."

"That's the way it is, huh?" he said softly. "You're getting too big for your pants. Just because you've been

fucked a dozen of times you thing you're mother Teresa. Okay, sister, here it is." He smacked her across her face hard with his open hand, at the same time spilling saliva at her. "Get out! You are not the only fish in the sea. Mind you, before I met you, I was a full time country boy, I changed women like cloths, and though I treated them like dogs they still came. All women are dogs, I believed. You can do to a woman whatever you want, and as long as you give her a good bone, she will never go."[6]

"Now get to sleep and shut your trap. You ain't got anything under those legs better than any other women."

He got into bed and snapped off the lamp at his side.

She remained sobbing with rage on the cold floor.

Kabwe was no sucker. She knew there was another woman. Her cold, sullen face became grimly set. "Next day, I'll start something." She told herself.

That settled it. From that minute, Kabwe planned to dig more into Chinuel's life. She didn't know how but she knew she had to do it.

Kabwe waited until Chinuel left the apartment, then she began a systematic search. She knew Chinuel had no time to memories addresses. Somewhere, she was sure; she would find a clue that would lead her to his whore. Her eyes hard and set and her hands impatient, she went carefully through Chinuel's wardrobe. She turned out every pocket, but she found nothing. She went through

---

[6] See also; 'The Wisdom of a monk,' a poem written by Chibesa Emmanuel. The poem tells you more on how to tame a woman ('Mungwi Technical Secondary School poetry club, 2004-2006 intake.)'

his drawers, careful not to disturb anything, but again she was unsuccessful. The next day she tried, but to no avail. It was not until three weeks of hard labor, that she had a break.

Surriana walked lightly towards her bedroom, she closed the door and looked outside the window. In just a few minutes it had become much darker outside. She shut her eyes and imagined she could see the strong, darker features of her lover standing behind her. She could feel is warm, slightly smoky breathing on the back of her neck. His hands on her hips, feeling him press against her buttocks.

She opened her eyes. He was gone. Kalenga was gone, and she prayed to God that he would never return. She had loved Chinuel ever since the first time she had set her eyes on him and he had never done anything that hadn't endeared him to her. She had never cheated on Chinuel. Only this time, his last deal forced her to accept a company. For the all week he had gone out and though he used to call her every day, she still felt lonely and as a redress for that she had accepted Kalenga's company. Their passion had erupted out of nothing, like a forest fire, or like an explosion of body chemicals. It had recklessly consumed them both, until she was hurtling totally out of control towards emotional disaster.

The knock on the door made her start.

Surriana turned. No doubt it was a newspaper man delivering the evening newspaper. She walked as fast as a snake and flung the door open. She was not prepared for a young extravagant beautiful blonde in the black coat and nice looking boots. Although she was no taller than her, she seemed to fill the all doorway with her presence.

"Is your name Surriana," Kabwe asked.

Surriana was mesmerized by the snap in Kabwe's crooked voice.

"You said it right, anything I can do for you?"

"Chinuel's boyfriend?"

"Oh." for a moment she was flummoxed. Then a thought struck her. "My boyfriend, is it about Chinuel? Has something happened?" She asked, sounding preserved.

Kabwe didn't smile. "Pipe down, nothing has happened to your boyfriend. I should be obliged if you invited me in your pad. I will not take long." It was politely said, but Kabwe terse tone did not invite contradiction.

Surriana let her inside and closed the door, and indicated a comfortable looking settee. "Sit down."

Kabwe sat down and folded her arms across her chest.

"Do you know Kalenga Kelvin?" She asked half smiling and half seriously.

The sudden silence in the room was bewildering. Instantly Surriana felt her cheeks colouring. A thousand and one question that begged answering. "How did this young lady know?" Anyway, what did it matter? She could think of no reason, but still she sensed she was somehow in deep trouble.

On impulse she blurted: "No young lady."

The hint of a smile died on Kabwe's face. There was no outward sign that she was enjoying the cat-and-mouse game of interrogation. No hint that she held all the cards or that she knew all about the woman's affair with Kalenga Kelvin, that it had been she herself who had selected and engineered the tall and handsome Kalenga to play the role of Surriana's seducer. Or that it was her who had instructed Kalenga to plant the hidden cameras in the room. All these things Kabwe kept to herself. Instead she warned tersely: "Think very carefully before you repeat your denial."

"I said I don't, Kid." Kabwe said using strictly B movie dialogue.

"And flat 6, Linda compound, ever been there?"

Surriana knew what was coming for her, Blackmail, but she waited for Kabwe to spell it out.

"Never been there and I will never, not in this age bracket!" She said her voice full of hatred. "But can you please stop this hide and seek game of yours and say your prayers, I would like to take a nap."

"Well, since you want it straight, here it is. You have been having a secret affair with Kalenga and I have the evidence. Are you interested in buying the evidence?"

"Blackmail, is it?" She asked.

"That's the idea," Kabwe said with a sneer.

"I'm not interested. Beside, to me blackmail is just a nine letter word and anyone who does that to me is just a nine letter being."

"That is talking rich, but if you're not interested I'm sorry I will have to tell your Chinuel and make sure that he never wants to see you again."

Surriana felt angry and defensive. "Chinuel wouldn't believe a scrap like that, I hardly believe what I did myself."

"And with Kalenga Kelvin: To testify to your affairs?" Kabwe asked.

"It would be my words against his!" Surriana snarled.

Kabwe reached the TV set, switched it on, and pressed the disc in the DVD and the screen flickered into life. As the fuzzy image settled down, Surriana was horrified to recognize a close-shot of her own face, her mouth wide and eager to take the engorged penis in front of her. She felt sick with shame. Then suddenly, with startling clarity she saw her whole future going into a ruin, she saw poverty, and loneliness and that is the only two things she never wanted in her life.

"You see! It is either you pay or this goes to your boyfriend, whatever he is to you. And don't make any fuzzy about it, I have another copy hidden somewhere. Should I die; the other copy still goes to your Chinuel."

"Does anybody beside you and Kalenga know about this?"

"Sileki bamundala!" Kabwe answered in her mother tongue which she articulated very well. "Except for a small boy with the other copy of the video, I call the boy every day, and the day I shall not, the boy sends the other copy to your Chinuel. You get the photo now, right?"

"How much are you asking?"

"A car just. Make it Benz in model."

"I see. I will have it delivered in two weeks time. What is the address?"

"Zibazako 303, and make it sticky, all else."

Surriana put on her wanyafye smile, and shut the door.

CHAPTER 11

Who would have ever known that a lady as careful as Surriana would find herself behind bars one day? What Surriana feared most happened to her.

Well, why bother with the Details? What is important is that despite being careful with life, she one day found herself in prison. Anyway, just to give you a photo of how she found herself in that hole, I would begin by saying; "The genius family are the most mistreated, mainly because they don't follow what their better judgment voices them to do."

Surriana knew she was crazy to have anything to do with Chinuel. But Chinuel had the kind of tricks that could make a woman do almost anything he wanted. So, she found herself accepting his company-even though it was against her better judgment. What her better judgment didn't tell her is that Chinuel had so many enemies and one of them was hunting for him. Or that she would one day find Chinuel shot dead in her bed room and she would be implicated for his death. That of course, saved her from the disgust of paying to blackmail. Don't get me wrong, I don't mean Surriana was totally happy that Chinuel was dead. For lack of better terms, I would say, she was half happy and half sad. Blackmail is one thing, if not the only thing she hated on earth, and Chinuel was the one thing she loved most on earth. You get the Photo now, right?

Well, here is Surriana's trial in brief. But don't be bored if it gets a little longer, I will soon be over it, just pipe down, and enjoy the fun part of it.

"All raise, the state versus Surriana, his Honor Judge Justine Chibale presiding." The judge took his sit and looked toward the defense team. The court clerk stood up and then read the charge: "Surriana aged thirty of Dambwa North plot number 303, your honor, charged with a prima facie case of murder: It is alleged that Surriana shot Chinuel on 3rd, January................."

The judge asked her whether she pleaded guilty or not guilty.

Just before she would make a statement to the judge, a handsome gentleman from behind her rose up and stated affirmatively: "My client pleads not guilty, your honor."

"Are you representing the defendant?" the judge asked, looking at the indictment sheet.

"Yes your honor," he said half smiling.

"May I hear what qualifications you have to stand before my court, Counsel Layman Chiluba?" The judge asked looking at Chiluba.

"I hold a Bachelor of laws degree from 'Mwakole University' and I was admitted to the bar last week," he said gallantly.

The judge and the attorney general exchanged smiles. "And this will be your first case."

"Yes your honor," he said gallantly again.

"I see. Is your client aware of this?"

"Yes your honor," he lied.

"But she wants you to represent her, despite this being a capital charge?"

"Yes your honor. But only because my client does not have money to pay for a well experienced lawyer, and I am representing her under simple terms just," he admitted.

"And what are those terms if the court may ask?" The Judge asked.

"That she will be kissing me two times a day, and triple times on weekends, until the trial is over."

The all court room of Judge Chibale broke in uncontrollable pandemonium, "Kisses of the virgin!" They murmured. It was only after the Judge hammered the gavel that the exuberance subsided.

"So you have chosen this case to give you experience and popularity, counsel?" The attorney general asked.

He gave him a titillating look and then said, "Yes attorney general, and can I say how proud I'm to have you as the head of the prosecuting team? I am well aware; of the gracious and professional manner in which you conduct the prosecutions."

The attorney General beamed and all the other state lawyers failed to hide their teeth.

"I'm also proud to preside over your first case, Counsel Chiluba." The Judge said and then turned to face the attorney general.

"Do you have any objection to Counsel Chiluba representing Surriana, Attorney General?" The judge asked.

"None whatsoever your honor; although it is most irregular that un-experienced lawyer who has not even appeared in court before is asked to represent a client with the capital charge, in the end it must be a defendant's decision and not that of the prosecuting team that must be followed."

"Then, Let us proceed with the case in hand," the judge said in an acute voice.

When the prosecution and the defense teams returned to their places, the judge looked down at Chiluba. "Will you be applying for bail, Counsel Chiluba?"

Chiluba rose from his place, "yes, your honor."

"On what grounds, defense counsel?" The judge ruled.

"That my client has no previous records, and constitutes no danger to the public."

The judge turned his attention to the attorney general.

"Does the state have any objection to bail Mr. Mbao?"

"We most certainly do your honor. We oppose bail not only on the ground that this is a capital charge, but because Surriana also tried to take her life. We therefore contend that Surriana does not only constitute the danger

to society, but also a danger to herself. Besides she may try to leave the state's jurisdiction."

Chiluba shot up, and gave the attorney general a taint look. "I must object, your honor."

"On what grounds, defense counsel?"

"This is indeed a capital charge, so leaving the state is hardly relevant, your honor. And as in any case, granting her bail will give time to our prosecuting team to collect enough evidence and arrange the prosecuting witness in a most professional and systematic manner."

He sighed and then continued; "as cap 87 Of the criminal procedure act provides: 'If the bail is not granted to a person having a capital charge, he or she must have a hearing of his or her trial within fourteen days of his or her arrest.'"

He turned to face the chief inspector of police, Mrs. Kupela.

"Your honor, let me submit to this court that it has been fourteen days–fifteen minutes, ever since my client was arrested and detained."

Spontaneous murmurs broke out from the prosecution team.

"Is the submission about the detention of Surriana as given by the defense counsel correct according to your records chief inspector of the police?" The judge asked while still looking at Mrs. Kupela with probing eyes.

"The submission is accurate your honor," said Mrs. Kupela sheepishly.

"Any further submission Defense counsel?"

"No, your honor, I only wish to seek guidance on a small point of protocol from the highly learnt team of prosecution." Chiluba said with that confidence defense Lawyers have.

The judge looked puzzled, as did the attorney general.

"Any objection on the defense counsel asking guidance on a small point of protocol from you?" asked the judge.

"No your honor, in fact, the state welcomes it." He said in a matakalic tone," and then turned to Chiluba.

"I can't wait to hear your small point of protocol, Counsel Chiluba."

"Allow me to enquire from you attorney general, if I am correct in thinking that before the trial, the prosecution and the defense team should sit down and come up with a list of twelve juries and two alternatives. And because of arguments, counter-arguments and several objections involved in the selection procedure, it could take at least a minimum of fourteen days before a trial date is fixed."

"That has been our normal practice, defense counsel." Mr. Isaac Mbao said, no longer puzzled.

"Then, may I assist my learned counsel by making it clear that should this court not grant my client with the capital charge a bail, then the trial should not be no later than tomorrow, as you know my client has already been detained more than the Criminal procedure act allows."

"But that's practically impossible, Defense counsel," the judge said looking perplexed.

"*In that case your honor, the only solution is to grant my client bail, unless it is up to the best interest of the court to break the laid down judicial protocol.*"

"*It is not in the best interest of this court to break the laid down judicial protocols,*" said the judge. "*So, I must now ask you attorney general,*" said the judge, turning his attention back to Mr.Mbao, "*is it in your intention to make any further objection to the granting of the bail to Surriana.*"

The court's attention swung to the attorney general and the state lawyers, all six of whom were in a huddle, holding an animated conversation. Judge Justine made no attempt to hurry them, and it was sometime before Mr. Isaac Mbao rose from his place.

"*We do believe your honor that it is no longer in the state's best interest to object the granting of Surriana the bail.*"

"*Bail granted,*' said the judge, and brought his hammer down. "*This court is adjourned sine die–until the twelve juries have been selected by both the defense and prosecuting teams.*"

"*All rise.*"

Within three minutes, the papers for a bail were signed, a sum total of three million kwacha was paid and Surriana was released on bail.

Mr. Justine Chibale winked as Chiluba and Surriana left the courtroom.

"*Sucker, how did you find yourself here?*" Surriana asked when they were outside the courtroom.

"So you haven't changed your bad manners of addressing me by awful names," Chiluba said in a kabandalic voice.

"Last time we met, you told me you're a sales man."

"I change careers like cloths my dear kid," he said happily. "Mind you, I'm a man with six degrees to my name."

"And what fool could like to sign such an agreement?" She asked after a moment's pause.

"Then count me out."

"But I haven't any money with which to hire a lawyer and even if I had, I don't think I may find anyone willing to take up my case."

"Then you have to represent yourself in court."

"But I don't have any knowledge of the law."

"Then be sure of being sentenced to death or being sent to Mukobeko prison for fifteen years or for life."

"But I didn't kill him," she said putting on a hard face.

"You can tell that to the juries my flower and see how they will monk at you." He said and gave her a mulish stare!

Fear swept through her face. She felt like the marrows in her bones were drying up. She couldn't find enough saliva to soften her gullet.

"So I only have one choice," she said more to herself than to Chiluba.

"And the sweetest choice ever," he said to her mockingly.

"You mean there is no any other way out of this besides that," she asked probingly.

Without minding to answer her, Chiluba locked her hands with his, and hurried her toward the office of the state lawyer. They found him having a tête-à-tête with the chief inspector of police. In no minutes the agreement form was signed and Surriana took an oath to abide by it.

Two weeks after she was granted bail, the juries were sworn in and Friday the 21st was fixed as the day of trail.

Chiluba was the first member of the defense team to appear in the courthouse and Surriana was the last; accompanied by Ivony Bantubonse, her primary school classmate. Once in the courtroom, she felt a thousand eyes giving her accusing looks, but she finally took her place on the left of Chiluba.

"Good morning, sucker," she said.

Chiluba smiled in a way that exposed all his right molars.

"I'm glad you haven't lost your sense of absurdity, but once the judge is in, I what you looking serious and concerned, a woman to whom a great injustice has been done."

"All raise, Judge Justine Chibale presiding." The court clerk said.

The judge invited the attorney general to make his opening statement.

Mr. Isaac Mbao rose from his place. He was wearing a dark blue suit, a white shirt and a blue tie. This was not un-usual of him; he always wore this attire on every opening of a trail because he believed it instilled a feeling of trust.

"Members of the jury," he began. "In all my five years as an advocate, I have never come across a more open-and-shut case of homicide as this one."

He turned his attention away from the judge and looked directly at Layman Chiluba. "In a few moments' time, defense counsel will rise from his place and with his famed charm and oratory will attempt to bring tears to your eyes as he tries to explain away what happed in that house. What he can't explain away is that the body of the deceased was found in Surriana's house."

The attorney general transferred his gaze on to the juries. "I can well understand you're feeling some sympathy for this lady, but after you have heard all the evidence you will be left in no doubt of Surriana's quilt and you will have no choice but to carry out your duty to the state and deliver a verdict of guilty.

There was an eerie silence in courtroom 3 when Mr. Mbao resumed his place. Several heads nodded, even one or two on the juries. Judge Justine Chibale made a note on the pad and then looked towards the defense counsel's table.

Do you wish to respond, defense counsel? Asked Judge Justine Chibale; making little attempt to hide the irony in his voice.

Chiluba rose from his place and looking directly at the judge. He said, "Only a brief opening statement your honor."

"Members of the jury," he began a slight tremor in his voice. "You have listened to the persuasive advocacy of the attorney general as he poured venom on my client, so perhaps the time has come for the prosecuting team to prove beyond reasonable doubt that it is indeed my client who killed the deceased, I what the prosecuting team to give prima facie evidence that my client had a hand in this murder."

"Are you through defense counsel?" The judge barked.

"Yes your honour, as I said it was a brief opening statement just." He said and regained his sit.

Chiluba and Surriana sat in silence looking directly in front of amidst the pandemonium that broke out in the courtroom. The judge banged his gavel several times, trying to bring the proceedings back to order. Chiluba glanced across the attorney's table; only to see Mr. Mbao, his head bowed, in a huddle with his prosecution team.

The judge tried to hide a smile once he realized what a shrewd tactical move defense counsel had made; it had thrown the Prosecuting team into disarray. The judge turned his attention back to the team for prosecution. "Attorney general that being the case, perhaps you'd like to call your first witness, the judge said mockingly. "It is just a matter of fact," he added as an afterthought.

Mr. Mbao rose from his bench, less confident than he was at his opening statement.

"Your honor, our prosecution team expected a lot of objection from the defense team. Again, we expected a long opening statement; unfortunately none of the two happened. In this unusual circumstance your honor, I would like to seek an adjournment."

"Is your witness not the chief inspector of police," the judge asked atomically.

"Yes your honor, we did not want to take her away from her import duties until it was proved entirely necessary.

Chiluba was on his feet; "objection your honor!"

"Sustained!" the judge barked.

"It is entirely necessary that the chief be present at all stages of prosecution because this is a murder trial, I therefore ask this court that this case be closed on the ground that there is no police evidence to place before the juries."

"Nice try counsel," said Judge Justine, "but I won't fall for it. I shall grant your request attorney general. I shall reconvene this court immediately after the lunch break. And if the chief of police is unable to be with us by then, I shall dismiss this case following the defense counsel's advice."

"All rise," said the court deputy as the judge glanced at the clock before leaving the courtroom.

After lunch break, the magistrate room of the honorable Chibale was crowded with the curious; the press, business men, accountants and a small army of lawyers who had more important things to do but just happened to be in the neighborhood. They all milled about and spoke in grave voices while keeping anxious eyes on the media. Cameras attract businessmen, accountants and lawyers like blood attract sharks.

Beyond the railing that separated the players from the spectators, Mr.Mbao stood in the center of a tight circle of his assistants whispering and frowning as if they were planning an invasion. He had changed into a dark three-piece suit, black shirt, red tie, and white shoes that shined to a glow. He faced the audience but of course he was too preoccupied to notice anyone.

Across the way, Surriana sat with her back to the gaggle of onlookers and pretended to ignore every one. Chiluba sat on the edge of the defense table, also facing the press while engaging himself in a highly animated conversation with a paralegal officer.

The court clerk stopped in front of the bench and yelled instructions for all to rise; "court is now in session, honorable Justine presiding." Judge Justine appeared from a side door, and was escorted to the bench by an assistant carrying stakes of heavy files. They sat at the middle of the twelve juries.

In his early forties, Judge Justine Chibale was a nonsense type, always typical-all business and hated prosecutors who were babies at law. He had started is law practice at the age of twenty and rose through the ranks from district attorney to magistrate judge. So, when the chief constable of police didn't show up to give evidence, he allowed the prosecution team to go on with the prosecution, but when the time came for judgment, he ruled in favor of the defense team. At least, you would call it that because Surriana was only given one year-six, instead of the maximum sentence of fifteen years usually allotted to murder in Zambia. To this he explained while passing judgment: "the maxim of 'rispsa loctuir' (things speak for themselves) does not apply here. The prosecution team has managed to convince the court that Surriana was in the house–her house for that matter, when Chinuel was murdered, but they have not shown us any police evidence to prove that it is indeed Surriana who killed Chinuel. But if we let every criminal go free just because the prosecution team is loose, then, prisons will be empty in a short while. Thus, though this court finds Surriana guilt, the court as only given her one year six months imprisonment with hard labor."

This page is intentionally left blank; it is for you Surriana Chanda Kaluba (not her real name). Thanks for taking a photo with me on the front cover of this book. And thanks for your express permission for it to be used as a cover photo of this romantic novel. Anyway, what are friends for, if not to make us celebrities?

CHAPTER 12

Forgive me if I sound sour. Surriana had to kill Tricia and escape from that prison; after all, it was not her fault. Tricia had to be silenced, she knew too much to be left alive while Surriana was out there enjoying her freedom. The police would have worked on Tricia until she had vomited all what she knew about Surriana. During those three boring weeks in that prison, she had come to confine in Tricia, Tricia was her true friend and she hoped they would escape together. But as time went by it became authentic to Surriana that Tricia did not have enough guts to face the world as a run-away convict. Prison life had taught Surriana a simple maxim of life: "life is very unfair; you can only make it fair by being very unfair to others."[7] Surriana would not imagine herself going back to spend any more days in that awful and dreadful place, worse still, sharing a cell with those beasts, sex-mongers,

---

[7] See also the same quote in 'Third Testament,' by the same author. All rights reserved.

malodorous punks, and self-centered characters. So, she killed her, not that she liked it, but she had to do it.

When she had escaped from that prison at 06:44hrs, it was raining cats and dogs; fit enough to drown an elephant. She ran in the pavement of the highway with a pretty odd sensation. She ran a few yards then paused to get the feel of freedom; she didn't feel like going anywhere. She just stood on the edge of the side walk, feeling the rain against her learnt face and letting the fact sink that she was now free. The rains made puddles in the road. It beat down on her prison raincoat: Warm rain, coming from a cloud swollen sky, as bitter as her.

Three weeks in that hole with female-child-rapists, thugs and murders with habits that would sicken a pig did something to Surriana. It had given her a hard heart, a dangerous heart, a heart as explosive as a volcano. It was a heart full of hatred and desire for revenge; not only for Chinuel, but for anything with balls. Every day, inside that wall; her heart kept boiling with increasing degree of hatred for Honcy, Chiluba, Chinuel, Kalenga and the whole of the male race.

She knew Chinuel was long gone, and that Chiluba had skipped from sight. But to the devils good luck, Honcy was still alive and within reach. While still in prison, Surriana had made plans to secure her future and somehow get a hand on Honcy. It was one of those plans she never liked, but she had to go through it. She had managed to acquire a Passport and a new National Registration card in the name of Susana, Honcy's wife. It hadn't been easy *to make those arrangements, but at last she succeeded. The permanent secretary at home affairs happened to be the ex-girl-friend to Honcy and like Surriana, she was looking for an opportunity to even scores with him, for dumping her like toilet tissue after using her.*

Immediately Surriana had reached Kachacha guest house, she had distinguished herself as Susana. Luck her, of all the people she could impersonate in the late mornings of first July, Susana seemed to be the easiest: Susana liked wearing a close-fitting canary tinted sweaters and white dresses, she had solid heavy hips and her dresses were tight fitting. She liked putting on bottle green sun goggles which concealed her face. She was about thirty; a blonde with nice long legs, somewhat seductive features, and as a general ensemble, she was very attractive to any man.

By the time Susana accompanied by a rather flustered solicitor had succeeded in making an appointment with the Chief Detective Inspector of police for the purpose of telling the police that she was being impersonated and she wanted it to stop; Surriana had extracted a total of ten thousand kwacha from Susana's account, transferred it to her foreign account, purchased clothes and furniture in Susana's name, posted them to Nakonde and sent her the bills. The cashier of that bank was somehow a mug. He had queried the signature on the cheque, but she had told him she had injured her wrist and had difficulties in writing normally. Because Susana drew up a lot of water at that bank, she had cashed the cheque and luckily, it did not bounce. The next escapade was when she appeared at a lucrative restaurant which the real Susana had patronized for years, ordered the most expensive food and the finest wine, and asked for a bill to be sent to Susana's residence.

Most unfortunately, Surriana got too tipsy; she did take a chance, she left the restaurant and made it to Honcy's dwelling place.

There was a long pause while she stared at the bungalow. The bungalow made her eyes nearly fell out of her head. It had nice lawns, a rose garden, a nice park, two swimming pools and a fish pond–as a general ensemble, the whole of it was classic and magnificent.

She felt really bitter. "If I had not taken Chinuel's offer, I would not be a run-away convict and being wanted for murder. Probably I would have owned a house as nice as Honcy's." She thought. "I know I'm just trying to sound off," she continued thinking around. "No woman could have refused such an offer; I did the right thing, only that the cards were stacked against me."

Just as she jerked the door open; she came face to face with Honcy. His broad fleshy face was alight with excitement at the sight of her. He stared at her; the stare was without any inhibition.

A wave of desire for revenge swept through her and like someone possessed with a demon, she saw her opportunity to get even scores with Honcy. She immediately planned to use Honcy as an instrument of pleasure, abuse him and make him pay for what he and Chinuel had made her go through. *"To forgive a wrong is to expose your weakness,"*[8] She muttered to herself.

"What a darling!" Surriana said in Susana's voice and smiled for Honcy immaculately.

"Welcome darling," he said leading the way to the bedroom.

Having reached the bed room, Honcy turned and faced her.

"I missed you darling, a lot of it," he said while taking off his hat and raincoat. She listened to all this with a tension that made her muscles ache–she felt bile being secreted in her stomach with increasing pain. While she made the bed, he went over to the window and lit a cigarette. Luck enough, he kept his face looking outside. She knew she had lost colour and she was sure he looked suspicious.

"Perhaps, he already know I'm not Susana," Surriana said to herself. *"And what if, then am sunk. The dice is surely loaded against me."* she thought.

There was a delayed silence while Honcy prowled around the dark room. Then he came toward her. He hesitated for a brief moment, mashed out the cigarette and then moved toward her, his heart was pounding fast.

She threw her arm around his neck. What followed was a spark of kisses between them. Honcy was an animal at it. He sucked her saliva until he felt her mouth become dry. His bilabials buzzed around her mouth with increasing passion, while his tongue was quarrelling

---

[8] This quote is taken from 'The Third testament,' all rights reserved.

with hers. As a general ensemble, the kisses were deep and lingering. Then, without a warning she produced a knife and stabbed him.

The violent ringing of the bell door put Surriana into panic; in as short as chicken sex, she went to the window and jumped slowly and carefully. She ran briskly, like snakes' business, until she found some place safe enough to hide.

At the far distance she heard the chief Constable of police assuring a bunch of Journalists: "We're playing a hunch that Surriana is still in this house. If she is not in this house then she could be hidden somewhere close and we are going to find her. Every house, every apartment, every farm and every street will be searched pedantically. We have plenty of men. It will take time, but if she's within fifty miles from here, sooner or later we'll find her. The organized search for her has swung into its stride and it is on the scale that will have her scared. Every road out of town is blocked. Army personnel from a nearby camp have been called in to give a hand. More than a thousand men, police and troops have been allotted territory in the needle-in-a haystack for the missing prisoner. Three helicopters are buzzing over the city with a direct radio link to headquarters."

As Surriana came from hiding and reached the main road; rains started falling like holy tembalake's business. A glittery BMW slide up beside her and the electrically driven off-side window rolled down. The car door swung open and as Surriana bent to stare in at the driver, a nice looking gentleman grinned at her.

"Come in. You're getting wet," he said.

She hesitated, and then a thought cropped in her. "No cop would ever dream of looking for me in this glittering BMW and with such a 'shatter of women' like him."

She got into the car and slammed the door. Her highly learnt eyes showed as nothing else could have pleased her than being invited for a ride. He grabbed her hand and squeezed it. "How are you, miss?" he asked.

"Cut out that miss paraphernalia. Mind you I'm not missing anything; I'm as perfect as rains. You call me Surriana, and you?"

"Saina, but you did not answer my question," he said, his smile slipped a little and his eyes searched her face.

"I'm alright," she said disentangling her hand from his.

"Don't tell me I'm getting a free ride."

"Sure, what are your plans?" He asked abruptly.

She was irritated to feel the blood rise to her face. "I haven't any, I want to look around the streets, and then have a cup of coffee at any decent restaurant."

"I was also thinking of having coffee. How about going to my place right-away? It is near, and besides it will save you a little bit of money."

"I've had a pretty of rough time before, just refusing a man's offer," she said more to herself than to him.

"I see, I'm sorry….. I didn't know."

"How would you?"

He grinned and shifted into gear. The BMW drifted away into the high way.

"Is this yours," She asked while looking at the ornate dash board.

"You bet. I bought her a couple of months ago. She is a honey, isn't she?

"So you certainly know how to keep yourself well heeled." She said and pulled on her don't forget me type of a smile.

"Sure!" He said and smiled fully, living his white teeth naked.

Saina pulled up outside the front gate of the police headquarters. When Surriana realized what was happening, a pistol was pointing at her. "You are under arrest. Anything you say will be used against you in the courts of law." He barked in a police voice.

"A clever trap, I didn't know the modern police officers can be all that sharp." She said to herself.

"This is the end of your run, Surriana. Back in prison, that is where you belong." He said as he was putting handcuffs on her. "And what a break, I have been waiting for this opportunity for nearly six years. I'm now happy I had waited so long because the take is big. With this arrest I will be promoted to the position of 'inspector of police.'"

"And what will become of me," 'Surriana asked.

"She that walks with a sword dies by a sword." He said and pushed Surriana out of the car.

"This life is very unfair, she said, I go back to prison and you get promoted for it."

"Who said anything about life being fair?" The sooner you realize that life is very unfair the better. In facts, if you want life to be fair, you have to be very unfair to others."[9]

"That is being even more unfair, quoting Chibesa Emmanuel's 'third testament' on me." Surriana said as he was putting her inside the police cells.

One thing that was odd on this particular day is; the police headquarter was disserted. Nearly all –if not all police officers were booked in the hunt for Surriana–the missing prisoner, a murder and a bank robber.

Before Saina could leave, Surriana pulled on him the oldest trick in the world. She stripped naked and said: "Come on! Untie me we make love."

Looking at her like that, Saina's mind was dazzled. He especially liked her luscious thighs and the Triangular shape of her leftovers. His penis abruptly erected and he ejaculated.

Promise me that you will allow me to have you once I reach you in safety.

"I Promise. And remember, a promise is real." She said.

"I can't wait," Saina said as he undid the handcuffs.

In as short as chicken sex, they were away from the police Headquarter and in safety. Passing the three roadblocks erected by the police didn't prove difficult to Saina, given his position in the police service. Saina had taken Surriana to his exclusive villa in the mountains.

---

[9] See also the same quote in 'Third Testament; the Gospel of money' by the same author. All rights reserved.

Apart from its constructer, no one knew about it. It was belt underground and unnoticeable. In the past he had used it as a love nest.

It surprised Surriana that Saina had not made any sexual advances for the first two weeks they had stayed in that Villa. Saina had asked for a Local leave, telling the boss that he had a funeral. However, just after a fortnight in that exclusive villa, something happened that changed the records. As they were drinking brand and listening to good music, Saina pulled Surriana to her feet and danced with her. Surriana's buttock quivered when she danced. Saina whispered to Surriana: "I'm famous for the size of my dick, you know, it makes women cry like pigs about to be slaughtered. You'll soon be introduced to it. And I hope for your sake you'll quiver as good as you have just done."

Surriana drew away and folded her hand on her breasts, and almost for the first time in the two weeks that she had been with Saina, she smiled. Because Surriana's smile was so secretive, it looked like a 'bride's smile of triumph.' Then, Saina picked up Surriana in his arms and, stumbling, carried her to the small fixed bed.

"Put me down," Surriana said.

But instead of setting her on her feet, Saina tossed Surriana into the air like a child and caught her by the rib cage when she came down. She gasped in pain. Saina gave her a rough kiss on the mouth, licking the underside of her upper lip. His tongue was as muscular as the rest of him, and to Surriana, its temperature seemed hotter than was human.

"*Stop! Stop kissing me that way,*" *Surriana said, but she hadn't the breath to say it loud enough for Saina to hear. He had drunk too much brandy to hear anything. He threw her up again, very high this time, above his head, and when she came down with her hair shimmering in the amber light from the exit door, he caught her in his strong arms and sank her on the bed, covering her face with kisses.*

"*Ah, Surriana, Surriana, my Surriana,*" *he moaned, "I love you so and much.*"

Surriana held her breath and closed her eyes, but she couldn't prevent all her senses from working, so she still heard Saina's muffled voice and smelled his breath and felt his maladroit hands on her body.

Saina lifted Surriana's foot, with the slippers still on, he kissed her foot while murmuring her name over and over, then, he kissed her ankle. She felt like the all of her leg had been sunk into a blast furnace.

"*You are burning me.*" *She said languidly.*

"*Saina did not listen to her. Shoe by shoe, stocking by stocking, ribbon by ribbon, he undressed her.*

"*No,*" *Surriana said, "no.*"

But again Saina did not hear her. Surriana tried to squirm away but he seized her ankle and peering along the inside of her left leg with one eye closed as if sighting a ghost and gave her a silly grin. Surriana did not want what was going to happen to her to happen. Watching Saina's dazed face, she began to form a plan of escape. She stopped protesting and stopped squirming. She lay on her back, limp and silent, while Saina removed her garments one by one. At last she was naked.

When Saina saw Surriana for what she really was– the luminous skin, her delicious breasts, her inviting leftovers, the onion shaped back, and her luscious thighs–he could not believe his eyes. The sight of Surriana and her generosity in letting him see her naked left Saina breathless. He had had hundreds of prostitutes and a good many unfaithful wives, but he had never before seen a nude female body; even with whores, even in the middle of the act, it had always been a matter of groping under shifts and peeking under hems.

"Lovely, lovely," he cried, tearing off his shirt. "Holy Tembalake, my friend come and look at what have caught, for you here." He said as if telling someone besides Surriana.

"What have I walked into?" He asked himself. "This is all women; the most sensual, sexual body I have seen."

She opened her eyes with a start. "Had he brought a friend into the room?" She asked herself.

She turned quickly and looked around, but there was no one. Then, she saw what he was talking about and remembered is words: "I'm famous for the big size of my dick," he had said, and indeed it was a big sized dick.

Surriana held her breath, opened her mouth wide, and bit Saina on his arm. In the first instant after the pain traveled from the point of injury to Saina's brain, he did not seem to comprehend what was happening to him. The pain was excruciating, but he could not believe that *it was actually coming from the part of his body it seemed to be coming from. Then, realizing the truth, he bellowed in amazement and thrashed so violently on the bed that he nearly pulled Surriana's teeth out of her jaw. He seized her head between his hands, and feeling the strength in his great blunt fingers, she thought that he might crusher her skull. She hung on like a rat, tasting salt.*

After a moment, Saina's muscles stopped obeying the commands of his brain. His hands relaxed and he stroked Surriana's hair. He spoke her name. He gasped. His body arched, twitched, and then went limp.

Surriana knew her plan had worked. He was helpless. But Surriana knew, too, that this condition would only last for a moment. She slipped of the bed.

"Jesus, Surriana," Saina said, and coming from him the sound seemed tinier, even, than it was. There was admiration in his voice.

"It is true that people we love do note love us as much us we do," he said to her.

"Surriana, You can't do this to me, not after what I have done for you; look at that painting on the wall." He said, now a little noisier than at first.

Surriana looked at the freshly painted portrait of an extravagant beautiful and stunning naked woman, that hung on the wall, Surriana knew it was supposed to be a picture of her because of its resemblance. Not because Saina had seen her naked body before, he had imaged it all from his head.

A wave of love swept through her body as she looked at the naked painted picture. She wouldn't imagine the picture was painted by human hands. It resembled her so much that it looked like a photo taken by the camera.[10]

During those two boring weeks, Saina did nothing except listening to good music while painting Surriana's picture. And if he is not doing that, he liked nothing but looking at Surriana; admiring her delicious body, her well calculated morphology, her nice long legs, her well curved behind, Her well pointed breast, her dove like eyes, and her inviting lips.

"Whoever had painted that picture must be an angel," she said.

"You love it," Saina said weakly.

"Yes, but not more than I love the painter," she said and smiled provocatively. She had loved Chinuel and still felt something for him, maybe because he was the first, as they say; "the first cut is the deepest." But the way she was now feeling for Saina was different. It was a mixer of sympathy and empathy. She felt really weak, a wave of paralysis swept through her bone marrows as she looked closely at the picture.

Saina saw that he had won the first move. "Time to throw my last card," he said to himself and looked apologetically at Surriana.

"Will you marry me," Saina asked Surriana.

---

[10] See also a painting entitled 'Surriana' at Malcolm Moffat college of Education By Chibesa Emmanuel (2009 to 2010 art work).

Without answering, she crossed the gap that separated them and Kissed Saina lethargically on his lower lip until he felt like the lip was on fire. As a general ensemble, she had kissed him like she was demented-tearing his tongue and chewing it like gums. She had offered herself to him like it was the only natural thing to do. He had taken her in the only way he knew to take women: Touching every part of her body methodologically and when he entered her, she had cried like a train whistle. He had entered her with the usual; the front, then the back door, and lastly with her on top of him. After he had culmed, he rolled off and slept by her side. She didn't do what most women do, but allowed him to hold her closely while kissing his bare chest.

From that day onwards, Saina made love to Surriana any time he felt like, until she became pregnant. And by the time things had cooled down and she was free to go where she liked without thinking that the corps will be on her, she was six months pregnant. You would think Saina married Surriana, not so? Well, you are in for a shock. As soon as Surriana announced to him that she had missed her period, Saina did what most men do; he packed and left her. Bad still, without even saying bye.

Another surprise, you believed Chinuel was shot dead, right? Worry not; a starling never dies in the story; that was just one of Chinuel's tricks. They killed the wrong guy, is double should I say, or rather a person who looked exactly as him. How two people could be as similar as that, nobody knew, that was Chinuel's secret. In fact, it was Chinuel who planted that body in Surriana's house, to give himself enough time to pull that deal. Don't get me wrong, I don't mean Chinuel deliberately killed his double. But after he found his double dead, he took his body and planted it in Surriana's house, a claver trap not so?

EPILOGUE

Now that you have came to the end of this highly erotica and romantic novel; what you might be wondering is that: is this story really true? And if it is as true as the writer claim it is, what does it contribute to modern society? Well, the later is a billion dollar question. I wrote this one to the world for two reasons. The First reason is for entertainment and culture preservation. The second one is to inspire people especially young ladies to be like Surriana; to struggle and stand up for what they believe in no matter what might come their way. And as the bible says in Proverbs 26:24, "he who speaks the truth kisses nice lips." Never be slow in saying the truth. Always remember that your best stories will come from your struggles, the seeds of your successes are in your failures. Your praises will be birthed from your pains. If you are in a jam like Surriana was in, read this book, have fun and keep in mind that there has never been a storm that lasted forever. Seasons changes; stand up and make the best out of life.

Other books by the same author

1. <u>*Third testament; the gospel of money*</u>
   Contain 365 contemporary secrets of the rich, a song of sorrows and a romantic true story.
2. <u>*Making the best out of life.*</u>
   Tells you the meaning of life, and introduces you step by step to Chibesa Emanuel's practical philosophy of 'making the best out of life.'
3. <u>*The poor in my pocket*</u>
   Tells you 100 reasons why most poor people are poor, will die poor, and the best thing you can do for them.
4. <u>*Umulembwe Wachipuba (Bemba Version).*</u>
   Aka katabo kalanda pali ba Chibesa Emmanuel beene. Pa mifyalilwe yabo, amasambilo yabo elyo nemyangalile yabo. Kanshi kuti twatila; ni autobiography yabo mucingeleshi.

KISSES OF THE VIRGIN

What makes 'kisses of the virgin' sensuous, irresistible and compelling to read? It is Surriana! At the age of thirty, Surriana Banda had done everything an extravagant beautiful and stunning woman would do with men except surrendering her virginity. She liked the struggles in houses, cars, and hotels where she kept her nice long legs tightly crossed and submitted to everything except that one thing. She had been seriously warned at her initiation ceremony to have nothing to do with sex–until her wedding day. But one bright summer afternoon, she bumped into Chinuel, and from that time onwards mysterious things began to happen to her until she was forced to give up that one thing, that one thing she treasure most. Worse still, she was imprisoned, nearly blackmailed, sexually abused, impregnated and compelled to unbearable pain and Sufferings.

Printed in the United States
By Bookmasters